CREATIVE GARDENS

CREATIVE GARDENS

David Stevens

A Japanese-style garden in Britain

HAMLYN

Dedication

To those nurserymen and landscapers I have the privilege of knowing as friends

Acknowledgements

Line artwork by Cynthia Pow and David Stevens

Colour photographs

The *Daily Telegraph* Colour Library: 10 (Patrick Thurston), 163 (Dimitri Kosterine); Valerie Finnis: 86 (The Dower House, Boughton House); John Glover: 14 bottom, 78 top; The Iris Hardwick Library: 51 top, 102 right; Jerry Harpur: 2 (Alex Rota), 19 top right and bottom right (Geoff Kaye), 34 (Tryon Palace), 38 left (Dumbarton Oaks), 38 right (Barnsley House, Cirencester), 39 (Jenkyn Place), 42 left (East Lambrook), 42 right (Barnsley House), 46 top and bottom (James Johnson), 47 bottom (Yeomans, Oxon.), 50 top (Yeomans), 50 bottom (Simon Hornby), 54 (John Vellum), 58 top (John Vellum), 62 (Beth Chatto), 63, 67 (Douglas Wright), 74 (Great Saling), 75 (Beth Chatto), 78 bottom (Burford House), 79 (York Gate), 82 (Heslington Manor, York), 87 top (Simon Hornby), 87 bottom (Barnsley House), 90 (Heslington Manor), 91 bottom (Jenkyn Place), 94 top, 95 (Alex Rota), 99 bottom, 114 bottom (Heslington Manor), 118 top (Barnsley House), 119 (York Gate), 127 (Victor Shanley), 134 top left (Williamsburg), 134 bottom left (York Gate), 143 (Brook Cottage, Allerton), 147 (Dick Balfour), 150 top (Simon Hornby), 154 (Barnsley House), 159 top (Abbot's Ripton), 162 (Alex Rota), 174 left (Yew Tree Cottage), 174 right (Steve Anderton), 175 (Barnsley House), 178 top (York Gate), 178 bottom (Barnsley House), 179 (Valery Stevenson), 183 (Jenkyn Place); Maggie Keswick: 166, 167; Frances Lincoln Ltd: 126 (photograph by Tania Midgley); Peter McHoy: 26, 30, 31 top; Tania Midgley: 58 bottom, 98, 99 top, 106 bottom, 107, 135 right, 146, 150 bottom, 171 right, 158; Robert Pearson: 102 left, 171 left; Photos Horticultural: 70, 91 top (Beth Chatto), 106 top, 122 (Adrian Bloom, Bressingham), 123, 151, 170; The Harry Smith Horticultural Photographic Collection: 43, 51 bottom, 103, 118 bottom, 135 left; David Stevens: 19 bottom left, 22, 47 top, 59, 63 bottom, 66, 114 top, 115 right, 131; Syndication International: 14 top, 18, 130, 134 top right, 159 bottom; Elizabeth Whiting Associates: 6, 15, 19 top left, 23, 27, 31 bottom, 71, 94 bottom, 110, 115 left, 138, 142.

The publishers would also like to thank Rosemary Verey for her help, and the Antique Collector's Club for permission to reproduce the illustrations on page 53 from *Colour Schemes for the Flower Garden* by Gertrude Jekyll.

Published 1986 by
Hamlyn Publishing,
a division of The Hamlyn Publishing Group Ltd
Bridge House, London Road,
Twickenham, Middlesex, England

ISBN 0 600 30639 9

Printed in Italy

CONTENTS

INTRODUCTION

The number of gardening books published each year never fails to amaze me. The subject is, of course, enormous, ranging from the specialized culture of rare species to methods of crop cultivation and the altogether wider topic of garden design and construction. Many books look at individual subjects in great detail but fail to take an overall view of the complete garden, and sometimes this is justifiable, particularly when help is needed in a specific area. Many other books look at the structure of gardens, great or small, but over-simplify their subject to the point of blandness. It is one thing to gaze in rapt admiration at a splendid landscape but something very different to understand why and how it works.

Another problem with both gardening books and the gardening public is the fact that the subject is considered to be almost entirely the realm of the amateur. This is in part an historical problem in that professional landscape gardeners, and more latterly landscape architects, are a minority profession. The point is that such professionals are both trained and hopefully have a real 'feel' for good design, resulting in an inevitable move towards a better home and garden environment.

This book, instead of beginning with a concept and working through the design process towards a satisfactory result, turns the whole sequence round. Its starting-point is a number of unique gardens, all of them particularly attractive or successful; it moves from there through the philosophy, design – and not least the hard labour – that has made these compositions really work in both visual and practical terms.

There are almost as many good authors of gardening books as there are talented gardeners but not all of them can convey the subtleties in the picture of a garden as a whole. For my own part I have been lucky: I have worked my way through a lengthy apprenticeship in nurseries, garden centres, landscape contracting and finally through a formal training in landscape design, which is where I have stayed with growing enthusiasm for the last 15 years. My work takes me all over the United Kingdom and often abroad and I have the privilege of knowing many of the gardens and designers whose work is the substance of this book.

Most gardeners – and I use the term to include everyone engaged in horticulture – have very few secrets. This does not mean that their task is not a complicated one, or that they have created their gardens without talent: in fact, the reverse is usually the case. What it does mean is that when they meet, their exchange of ideas and their willingness to discuss them are usually spontaneous. In many ways this is why the idea of this book appealed to me from the start. It was a chance to find out why certain compositions worked so well and to investigate them in pleasurable detail. The reasons were often surprising, the results superb.

An architectural garden must have continuity. Here the various elements – the lamp globe, the subdued, subtle colour scheme, and the low maintenance planting – combine to make a very effective and unified image

THE IMPORTANCE OF A THEME

Gardens are often of a type: they cater for a particular requirement or revolve round a central theme. Good design, in whatever field, is usually single-minded and often simple. This does not preclude subtlety but it does eliminate over-complication. Fussy gardens of the kind that incorporate everything but the kitchen sink are a disaster and unfortunately, in this age of media advertising and proliferating garden centres and nurseries, the means to create them, however well intentioned, are increasing. Many of the gardens considered here have been created by professional designers who have not only drawn upon years of experience but also used that most valuable gift, sensitivity. Others are owned by plantsmen or plantswomen and rely upon a delicate balance of flower and foliage that provides interest throughout the year. Others are the inspired work of amateurs. The theme of all of them is compatibility with their owner and with their surroundings.

It is the element of personality that separates one garden from another. Six identical plots will all turn out quite differently, because each one will have imposed upon it quite separate demands. All six gardens may well be successful, but each one will be unique, as are the people who create them.

The real thing – the garden that fits the purpose for which it was designed – is born of inspiration. If success is directly related to strength of purpose, it follows that there are as many styles as there are individual requirements. This is the basic premise of the book; however, it does not deal with a random selection of gardens but follows a definite pattern.

Roofs and **conservatories** (pages 16 and 12) are directly linked to the house and if the garden, or at least part of it, can be treated as an outdoor room, then these two items are the first step into it. The next topic is the specialized but fascinating **Knot gardens** (page 36) which are followed by **Herb** and **Cottage Gardens** (pages 39 and 47). **Water** (page 55) in all its forms, from the tranquillity of a lake to the intricate workings of a millstone fountain, has an almost irrestistible appeal. The subject needs a certain amount of technical detail to explain how certain features are put together. This is more helpful than showing a finished picture but omitting to tell the reader how it was achieved.

To many people **Plants** (page 83) 'are' a garden, but as a landscape designer I know that this is only partly true. Another approach might be called **Architectural** (page 125): the composition relies rather more on 'hard landscape' materials, and especially on the use of sculptural plants to temper the precise line of paving and walling. Such gardens almost inevitably adjoin a building and at their best are the epitome of what can be called landscape architecture.

The mood and style of gardens is remarkably diverse. The **Japanese** (page 162) have a climate not unlike that of Britain but they have evolved a tradition in gardening that relies heavily on religious ceremony.

In Britain the only indigenous style was the great landscape school of the 18th century: just as the British are a blend of many races, so **English Gardens** (page 156) reflect a blend of many styles. Sometimes this is delightful – in a cottage garden for example. Sometimes, when it results in the worst suburban clutter, it is a disaster. Recently the trend in Britain has been to emulate Scandinavian garden design and also to consider seriously the practical outside rooms of the west coast of America. The result is a new and unique style of English garden design.

Colour (page 139) is a major factor in planting design and the idea of devoting a garden – or at least a part of it – to a single tint can be irresistible. White is always stunningly attractive, but so also are green, pink or purple. The greatest of plantswomen was **Gertrude Jekyll** (page 51), the first gardener to really investigate the colour relationships of flower and foliage. Since the turn of the century many of her favourite plants have been hybridized to show even better characteristics and it is quite possible to interpret her ideas in a thoroughly contemporary way.

Although most of us are confined to our own 'back yard' – or at all events to a garden of modest proportions – it is always a worthwhile exercise to look at settings on an altogether larger scale. **Woodland Gardens** (page 94) are a favourite of mine, as indeed they were with Gertrude Jekyll. They give pleasure to the ears as well to the eyes whenever a breeze stirs in the boughs of the trees or moves the long plumes of bamboo and grasses. A natural wood is generally full of bluebells and foxgloves and if it has acid soil may well contain rhododendron and azaleas.

Like the landscape that is continually being changed by the hand of man, gardens mature and are subject to whims. The underlying framework may remain the same but the outer details change. Lighting, pots, containers, statues and furniture increase the personal element in a garden; all of them need to be considered and they can make or mar the end result. Is it the light or the light-fitting that is important? Should pots be grouped or placed singly? What about growing vegetables in the herbaceous border?

Generally speaking, contemporary gardens are more adaptable to change than their grand forbears. The latter were usually laid out to an inflexible framework, the beds within such composition being earmarked for a particular type of planting.

These days houses and their gardens change hands far more frequently and although the underlying pattern may well suit a new occupier, the planting can often be reworked to provide a completely new character. It is of course exactly the same principal as redecorating inside the home.

Never copy a garden from this book or any other book: to do so would be to rob it of that unique attribute of personality. Look, by all means; analyse, certainly; but, above all, gather ideas that revolve round a theme that is right for you.

HOUSE AND GARDEN: A UNITY

Even in the grandest Renaissance gardens, filled with courtiers, an intimate atmosphere was always cherished. The 'giardino segreto' was a very special place to which the family could withdraw. Surrounded by walls and softened by foliage, it looked back to the Roman peristyle and forward to what is now called an outdoor room. It turned its back on a hostile world. Today, mounting environmental pressures and diminishing space on which to build make the link between house and garden increasingly important.

The way in which this link is made can, of course, vary and depends largely on the style of garden and space available. A hundred years ago, the new-found skill in the use of iron made conservatories all the rage. At that time they were not primarily a way into the garden, but a setting for collections of exotic plants, ferns and palms. Today their role has been reversed and their main function is to act as the transitional stage between the indoor and outdoor world. They are also a place to sit when the weather is not fine enough for the garden: the glass produces a greenhouse effect that suits human beings as well as plants.

Nothing in the last thousand years or more has surpassed the Persian glorietta (a courtyard garden) as a place for living out of doors. It was the setting for social life on a grand scale: its courts, set with trees and water, were the scenes of eating, entertaining and love-making.

The patio, another courtyard, is found all over the world but originated in Spain. Somehow the word has come to mean any paved area that adjoins a house (even the drab strip of concrete left by builders of new developments) but the correct term is really terrace, which can also mean a series of platforms at different levels. At its best a terrace subtly combines paving materials and include walls, seating and planting in a composition that makes a place to pause before entering the garden as a whole.

Size is in many ways unimportant, I have seen and created perfect outdoor rooms from the most miserable and squalid backyards. Equally valid, although very different, is a sweep of fine old stone paving ranged along the back of a period building.

Roof gardens are a thing apart: are they linked with the house or with the sky, or some point in between the two? Their design really depends on the access to them and there is attraction in the challenge to create a garden in perhaps the most hostile environment of all. Sometimes they are reached through a trap-door into a Mary Poppins world of chimney pots and flowers, sometimes the atmosphere is altogether more sophisticated – say, a penthouse apartment with ample outside space for cultivated beds, pots, seats and barbecues. Unity is always the key. It makes living in the garden natural and uncomplicated.

The garden as an extension of the house – the outside room – helped in transition by the conservatory and its planting

Conservatories

The dictionary defines a conservatory as a greenhouse for tender plants, and while this is more or less accurate, the uses of greenhouse and conservatory are, and always have been, rather different.

A greenhouse is used for the culture of plants; a conservatory is for showing them off. The latter is also a place in which to sit and entertain, the plant material being moved in and out of the room so that it always looks at its best. As early as the 17th century, greenhouses were used for entertaining in the summer, when the plants were moved elsewhere, and for horticultural purposes during the winter. Not until the mid-18th century were the two functions combined in the form of building that is familiar today.

During those early days, conservatories, particularly on the continent, could be as much as 100 m (300 ft) long. It was not so much the new technology in iron that led to the great increase in conservatory building in Britain, as the abolition of the glass tax in 1845. From then the fashion – for it was a genuine fashion – grew more and more popular, only starting to decline seriously about the turn of this century. Wrought iron, although popular, was also expensive, and many conservatories were built with timber frames. This means that only the best maintained of these have lasted; today's conservatories are of different construction.

Just as the word 'patio' is used nowadays to mean any paved area, so 'conservatory' covers any ramshackle, lean-to structure that has glass, perspex or even polythene as a covering. To my mind a conservatory must be something more than this.

The misnomer is almost entirely due to a form of horticultural snobbery, which runs parallel with the fashion for neo-Georgian homes. To 'have' a conservatory takes one up market in a depressing manner, far better to call it a 'lean-to' and leave it at that.

First and foremost, a conservatory should adjoin the house and give access to the garden, so that there is a real progression from indoors to

Although designed to a traditional pattern, this conservatory is of a type currently in production. Built of brick and timber, the panes can often be double glazed to maximise heat retention. Note that the paving has been kept square with the building, a far simpler approach than trying to match the underlying hexagonal shape

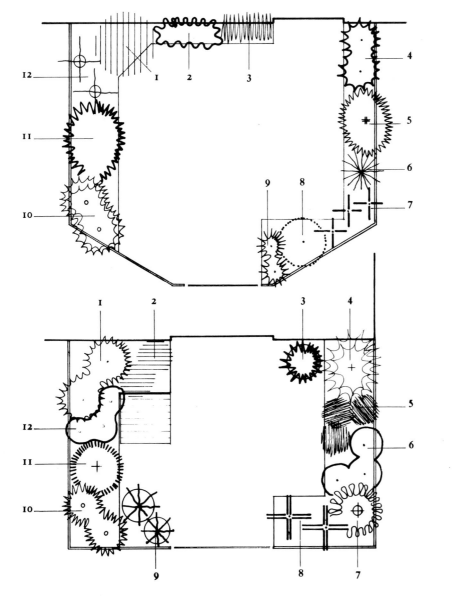

Key to planting plan

1 *Bougainvillea*
2 *Hibiscus rosa-sinensis*
3 *Jasminum polyanthum*
4 *Trachycarpus fortunei*
5 *Hibiscus rosa-sinensis*
6 *Prostranthera rotundifolia*
7 *Grevillea rosmarinifolia*
8 *Bletilla striata*
9 *Agave americana*
10 *Nerium oleander*
11 *Grevillea robusta*
12 *Nerium oleander*

Key to planting plan

1 *Rhodochiton atrosanguineus*
2 *Protea sp.*
3 *Agave americana*
4 *Phoenix canariensis*
5 *Prostranthera rotundifolia*
6 *Gerbera jamesonii*
7 *Tibouchina semidecandra*
8 *Clivia miniata*
9 *Strelitzia reginae*
10 *Bletilla striata*
11 *Tibouchina semidecandra*
12 *Trachycarpus fortunei*

outdoors. The perfect example of this is shown on page 10. A dramatic statement is made even more telling by the transition from a comparatively dark interior to a garden full of background interest. Added emphasis is provided by the centrally placed table in the foreground, the hanging fern and lastly the cleverly planted bowl in the garden itself. Any one of these focal points in isolation would have caught the eye too easily; but together they draw the seeing eye gently through the space with maximum effect. Another interesting point is that the whole structure is very simple: a timber frame with French windows (patio doors simply do not work in this setting), unobtrusive matting on the floor and comparatively few plants, placed symmetrically to reinforce the underlying pattern. The only criticism is that corrugated perspex for a roof, although cheap and easy to fit, makes a sound like thunder in heavy rain.

Planting is the next major factor, and in a conservatory the gardener has free rein with an enormous range of species, although the fact that they are

When planting a conservatory the imagination can take flight out of our temperate climate. Orange and lemon trees, bouganvillea and all kinds of exotics can jostle for pride of place. Watering and adequate ventilation are always controlling factors however, so remember that such places are far from maintenance free. These two planting plans utilise simple and easy to cultivate species that would look at their best throughout the year.

usually tender or half-hardy varieties limits the choice to some extent. It also gives many conservatories their Victorian atmosphere. Ferns, ficus, vines and many climbers are all popular. Remember that scent is an additional pleasure on a warm summer's evening – and so, too, is fruit that would be hard to ripen outdoors. In the conservatories shown here, the planting varies almost as much as the pots and containers in which it is grown. Technically there is little differences between conservatory and greenhouse conditions and the speed at which things can dry out is alarming, so the basic rule of the larger the pot the better works every time. There is nothing worse than going away for a few days, leaving well-intentioned neighbours to care for the plants, and returning to find them burnt to a frazzle. Over-watering is almost as bad: when it comes down to it most house plants are killed through kindness.

Plants set a theme, and so, too, does furnishing and decor. The conservatory at the top of this page is a modern addition to an older house. Again there is the the sensible use of French windows leading out from the building, and the conservatory has incorporated a brick garden wall on one side. The planting is relatively sober with a selection of palms, ferns and jasmine, but the whole composition has been given its own special atmosphere by the introduction of wrought iron furniture and the dramatic blue and gold jardiniere. The latter really acts as a punctuation mark in what is essentially a simple and low-key design. The floor is inexpensive vinyl, but in a traditional tiled pattern that adds rather than detracts from the overall picture. Floors are always an important consideration and the genuine tiles shown at the bottom of the opposite page are just right, in my view. The chequerboard pattern is geometrical to catch the eye, but its simplicity makes it a good background for the

Left and below: *I am reminded of a jungle fantasy whenever I walk into these fern laden rooms. Some of the most successful also contain aviaries, while the largest include collections of exotic butterflies*

furniture and those wonderfully comfortable, if creaky, wicker chairs. The planting, too, is lush without being brash.

In direct contrast is the plastic turf in the conservatory at Strawberry House. A lot of nonsense is talked about the sin against aesthetics of using imitation grass. It is simply carpet, and a hardwearing one at that. If it works, use it: it works very well here! In fact, a conservatory floor has to be practical, it takes a lot of wear, often from muddy shoes and frequently gets wet when the plants are watered. A tile floor is best of all, but modern synthetics are almost as good.

Flowers and foliage provide emphasis and interest. It is, however, worth noting that all the conservatories illustrated here are painted white. This is both traditional and practical, because it provides reflection and links sky and garden. I have seen a magnificent wrought iron building in which all the metalwork was painted black, but I must admit that this felt psychologically wrong. The delicate tracery of the iron work was instantly visible – and was, incidentally, superb – but it dominated rather than played a background structural role. The whole effect was not only wrong but eerie.

As a final attribute consider the fantasy element. To my mind a conservatory provides this too, particularly when lit up. Go into the garden at night and look back through the glass to a tracery of foliage that takes on an etherial quality when lit from within.

Conservatories may be a legacy from an age very different from that in which we live today, but their continuing popularity underlines the point that they are both attractive and practical. They are an ideal link between house and garden and they extend the time during which we can 'live outdoors' to virtually the whole year.

Roof Gardens

Roofs do not make ideal gardens. They are either very cold or very hot or racked by high winds, and they present all kinds of structural problems. However, they are often the only open space immediately available to city dwellers. Ingenuity and the wish to be surrounded by plants in an environment less alien than bricks and mortar have a way of diminishing the difficulties.

Although the style and location of the roof garden can vary from a penthouse to the tiniest balcony, the common denominator is the harsh conditions, limiting species to those that are native to dry, semi-desert or at least Mediterranean climates. One bonus – and there are not many – is that frost is less common in densely built-up urban areas and the choice of plants can take this into account.

Before considering the structural, access and other problems, there are two questions to be answered: is it all going to be worthwhile and what is really required from the space? Many roof gardens are a waste of a great deal of enthusiasm – and, incidentally, hard cash – in the long run because the inevitable high maintenance, in terms of watering and replanting, outweighs the pleasure of using the area as an outdoor room.

A roof garden may not be a place to sit at all, but a setting for the marvellous massed effect illustrated on page 18. This is really extraordinary: hardly a square centimetre wasted in the pursuit of foliage, bloom and scent. There is barely enough room to move, let alone sit down, but the effect is worth it. This is nothing short of paradise suspended above the city: truly a hanging garden.

However, basics come first and if the problems are understood, the

While conservatories linger nostalgically in the past, this roof garden is unashamedly modern. An uncluttered rectangular design radiates out from the central raised beds. Sun loving species are planted that are tolerant of dry, arid conditions. Remember that such gardens are usually built in the most hostile environments

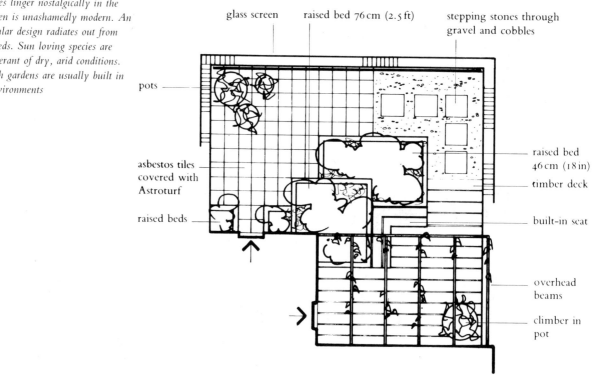

glass screen   raised bed 76 cm (2.5 ft)   stepping stones through gravel and cobbles

pots

asbestos tiles covered with Astroturf

raised beds

raised bed 46 cm (18 in)

timber deck

built-in seat

overhead beams

climber in pot

project is then well on the way to being a success.

The first essential is access. In many situations this is a straightforward matter and in new blocks of flats and apartments a substantial balcony or specific roof garden area is an integral feature. In older property, however, access can vary from narrow stairs to almost impossible trap doors, reached by dubious ladder arrangements. The latter may be acceptable for an occasional visit to mend the roof or install a TV aerial, but make regular access impossible. Since the construction of the garden will involve carting often bulky materials to roof level, it may be necessary to improve the way up by installing stairs.

Next, there is the matter of the structure of the roof. New roofs are usually built with considerable load-bearing potential: in other words, it is possible to create a garden with containers, soil and plants without fear of the roof collapsing. Old roofs, however, are very different, and so too are newer flat roofs that were never intended for anything more than a roll of bituminous felt. The timbers (and virtually every building more than 30 years old uses timber) were not designed to accept roof gardens and it would be advisable to ask the advice of a structural engineer before starting to create one. This does not mean, of course, that the timbers are not strong enough: it simply raises a question that should be answered sooner rather than later.

The answer to the gloomy questions – is it really worth all the time, effort, professional fees and worry – is the location itself. Despite the wind and possible vertigo, the roof gardener is in a different world. Views that can be so cramped and dull at ground level suddenly spread out to the

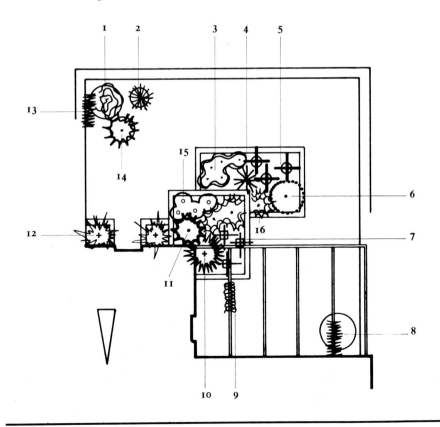

Key to planting plan

1	1	*Choisya ternata*
2	1	*Potentilla fruticosa* 'Tangerine'
3	5	*Helianthemum nummularium* 'Wisley Pink'
4	1	*Yucca filamentosa*
5	3	*Potentilla fruticosa* 'Red Ace'
6	1	*Phlomis fruticosa*
7	3	*Hebe subalpina*
8	1	*Lonicera japonica* 'Aureoreticulata'
9	1	*Clematis* 'Nellie Moser'
10	1	*Senecio* 'Sunshine'
11	1	*Genista lydia*
12	2	*Hebe albicans*
13	1	*Jasminum officinale*
14	1	*Genista hispanica*
15	4	*Festuca glauca*
16	3	*Santolina incana*

In this plan many grey foliage plants are used which are particularly suitable for windy positions. It is also interesting to note that the colours of the flowers has been kept within a relatively cool colour range. Garish colours can often look washed out in strong light so keep things as restful as possible

Above and opposite: *As roofs are often small they form the ultimate outdoor rooms. Style and content may vary but the underlying theme of intimacy and individuality is very apparent in all these examples*

horizon in unfamiliar and fascinating detail. Sun, sky and clouds create ever-changing patterns. The architecture of surrounding buildings is different, too, chimney pots, parapets, slates and tiles, all angled and positioned in odd ways that make the term 'roofscape' come alive.

When roofs are not so high, their problem may be rather more mundane, like those of the garage roof shown opposite: a boring expanse of concrete on the way to the front door. Whatever the situation, it can be exploited in a sensible and worthwhile way.

The first consideration in making a roof garden is shelter. In all the gardens shown here, shelter is either provided by the surrounding roofs or has been created by some kind of fence. It does not always follow that the higher the building, the stronger the wind, but it is a fact that a permeable screen that filters the wind rather than stopping it dead is the best choice. A solid wall or a plate glass screen may seem sensible but it will cause a great deal of turbulence that can make it almost impossible to sit in the garden. Even the simple plastic netting in the first balcony illustrated here, when it is clothed with plants, gives a remarkable degree of protection.

The next consideration is the floor. All too often this is either black felt, which is quite unsuitable, or those rather boring grey lightweight tiles. If the roof has the load bearing capacity, the floor plan could follow that on page 16. In this design I left the existing tiles in place and worked over them in a combination of stone chippings, cobbles and a sweep of green plastic turf. The composition is held together by the dividing lines of thin

brick paviors. The 'Astroturf' is ideal in this situation: light, maintenance-free and quite suitable for a whole roof area if necessary. Incidentally, the use of cobbles and chippings is similar to that on the garage roof. Here I took a straightforward paving slab as a basic module and infilled with the secondary materials, pots and planting. The whole scheme is cheap, practical yet attractive.

I once worked on the roof of a superb old river police station that had been converted into apartments. The views were breath-taking and the whole building had been constructed like a fortress. The roof itself was laid with fine old glazed tiles. The result was a unique outdoor room.

While many plants spring to mind when creating any outdoor environment do not forget that an interesting floor pattern can do much to provide interest where growing conditions are difficult

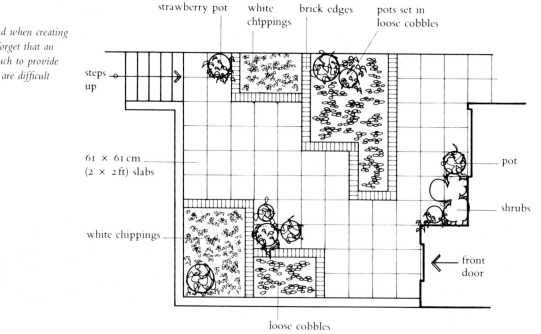

strawberry pot   white chippings   brick edges   pots set in loose cobbles

steps up

61 × 61 cm (2 × 2 ft) slabs

pot

shrubs

white chippings

front door

loose cobbles

It is planting that brings any garden to life and there are a number of options as far as containers are concerned. As in conservatory planting the bigger the pot the better, and if it is possible to incorporate raised beds, better still. As a general rule the strongest part of any roof is the perimeter, where the load-bearing beams below enter the walls. If you check with your architect or surveyor you may also find that walls span part of the area below and these might allow the positioning of a more central feature. Beds may be constructed from a variety of materials: timber, lightweight building blocks that can be rendered or treated with waterproof stone paint, or large fibreglass troughs. Drainage is important, as all these are, in effect, only big flower pots and become waterlogged if they have no holes at the base. When building beds, it is worth considering built-in seating, barbecues or overhead beams; the latter are particularly effective as shelter from hot sun. When considering the surroundings do not as a general rule paint them white. The result is too harsh and glaring. Cream or another muted colour is ideal. The beds should not be filled with garden soil. The task of bringing it up to the roof is too daunting and in bags in any quantity it is extremely heavy. I use a base layer of lightweight clay granules, topped with lightweight compost. This reduces the load very considerably and provides an excellent growing medium in which root systems can establish quickly. Of course, plants grown in these conditions take a lot out of the ground and need regular feeding to ensure that they maintain their development.

While raised beds provide ideal growing conditions do not forget pots entirely. Almost anything will do, provided it is big enough and with a bold foliage plant the container often becomes incidental. Style is, however, important and there is nothing worse than a bevy of Georgian chimney pots in an area of steel and glass. Apart from costing a fortune,

Pots are invaluable in any garden and particularly so on a roof. The range is enormous: always try to respect the underlying theme of the garden. Perhaps the most important point to remember is adequate size to ensure a cool root run and better growing conditions

brightly coloured smooth fibreglass containers would look far more handsome. In other words, respect the surroundings and you will feel comfortable.

Plants come last. They always do in any garden planning but they bring the whole composition to life. The planting scheme for a roof has to take extreme conditions into account, and provide either for seasonal interest that is at its peak during the warm summer months, or for a more balanced display that gives colour and interest throughout the year. The tiny balcony on the left of page 18 is the perfect example of instantaneous effect. African marigolds, begonias, agapanthus, coleus and fuchsia provide colour; roses, clematis and honeysuckle add interest and fragrance at a higher level. More permanent planting, which creates a backbone for the garden includes fatsia, bay and the blue-leafed conifer, all of which will hold the design together when brighter colour fades.

The two views of the same garden to the right of page 19 illustrate a more far-reaching planting plan. There is a higher proportion of evergreen or variegated foliage, the contrasting leaf patterns creating fascinating visual harmonies. The sumach, which is one of the better small trees for growing in a container, adds vertical emphasis and always looks dramatic, even in winter, when those gaunt branches take on a striking architectural line. This garden also blends gently into a surrounding street scene of green trees, softening the boundaries and creating a feeling of greater space.

A final note: chimney pots create an atmosphere of their own, particularly that fine old line of Victorian stacks forming the boundary to a quite delightful little garden on page 10. Sensible planting includes hebe and hypericum, cytisus, grasses and ivy, all of which love these dry, hot conditions.

Patios

The role of a garden is to provide enjoyment – through the cultivation of plants, lawn or vegetables, through the study of wildlife, through children at play or simply through being able to relax in private and congenial surroundings. The degree of garden maintenance will, to a great extent, be determined by the type and distribution of planting but the major item of expense in any garden is the hard landscape. Into this category falls paving in all its forms, walling, fences, steps, paths and drives. The patio or terrace will in all probability be the place where hard landscape is most important in practical, visual and financial terms.

The picture at the bottom left of this page shows a corner of a tiny patio garden measuring barely 6 m (20 ft) square. My brief was simple but daunting: I had to create a sitting area within the confines of a tiny estate garden. On either side ran bare, open, post and wire fences, while a sombre concrete block wall stopped the view abruptly, opposite the house. A small pool was called for, preferably raised, so as to deter a toddler and if planting, too, could be raised, so much the better. Almost instant maturity was important as the family might have to move at short notice and, above all, cost had to be kept as low as possible. In other words, it all had to be done on a shoestring budget.

As cost was a key factor I decided to use as many secondhand materials as possible and suggested to my clients that old bricks and floor boards might make a significant contribution. They looked doubtful until the boards, run through a planer, came out looking like a brand new ranch fence. As the terraced house was brick the well-baked, hard old stocks formed an ideal link between house and garden, creating a floor full of character. The same bricks were used to build the raised beds and pool, the latter being slightly tapered to fit the awkward splay of the boundaries. One end of the pool was bricked in to form a plinth, the perfect setting for

Both of these gardens are delightful examples of the garden designer's art. They occupy tiny spaces in a city environment and use a strong framework of brick, timber and paving slabs softened by intelligent planting that relies on the shape and texture of foliage rather than brash flower colour

a group of old terracotta pots filled with pelargoniums. The garden had a very slight change of level and in order to emphasize this, and so create two separate sitting areas, I constructed a broad brick step, turning the paving pattern at an angle to the lower level to give a visual warning of the drop. A statue should always have somewhere positive to go and the little Roman boy warrior sits comfortably at the junction of step and pool, gazing expectantly into the water.

A fence can have a powerful impact, but most of them are, in fact, exceptionally dull. The floor boards, nailed to hidden posts, produced a strong horizontal line, providing a sense of perspective that lengthened the garden considerably. They draw the eye to the block wall, painted white and softened by the foliage of maple and birch.

Planting completes the picture and such a positive design deserves an equally positive green covering. Planting patterns are discussed later, but to my mind the shapes, colours and textures of leaves can often be far more telling, and certainly last longer, than a quick flush of flower. Here the bold dracaena acts as a counterpoint to the architectural line of paving and walling, while hostas and alchemilla produce an altogether different pattern. On the other side of the steps a Japanese maple closes the gap with delicate fronds, the boulder adding a final, more natural note that compliments the statue at a lower level.

In many ways this is contemporary English garden design at its best: it owes nothing to those rather dubious styles from between the wars and looks rather for its inspiration to the gardens of Scandinavia and the West

Another outside room but in an altogether more relaxed style. The path and slight change of level lead both feet and eye to the secluded sitting area

Design should never be static in whatever field. This garden uses both traditional bricks and modern concrete blocks, both elements tied together into a series of overlapping rectangles. The seat provides unity, running around the pool and across the space. Perhaps the most important lesson to be learnt here is simplicity and clarity of style

Coast of America. It is, in short, both practical and pretty, two qualities of which we should never be afraid.

Throughout this book gardens of every conceivable kind are illustrated, the common bond between them being excellence. It is easy under the circumstances not only to take such work for granted but to look at the settings and feel that they are totally removed from your own backyard, idyllic and unattainable. In fact, nothing could be further from the truth. In this section most of the designs have been executed within the last few years, reaching maturity in a remarkably short time. Many were created in the most mundane situations and all, once established, need minimal maintenance. The fact of the matter is that good design caters for as many eventualities as possible and the idea that designers are mystical beings, conjuring inspired compositions out of the air, is nonsense. Any good designer works to a well-tried set of rules that are the product of experience and that achieve a satisfactory result. This, of course, never precludes originality and inspiration, but it does take a lot of the guess work out of a building a worthwhile outdoor room.

One of the first jobs a designer must do is to make the basic allocation of space and this will depend on a wide range of factors. As far as the paved sitting areas are concerned – and there may be several in a garden of even modest size – what is taken into account is access, sun, shade, shelter, changes of kevel and, perhaps most important of all, the budget available. It is, for example, quite obvious that a house facing north will cast a shadow over a considerable area in its immediate vicinity, or that a particular prevailing wind may make sitting out uncomfortable without shelter.

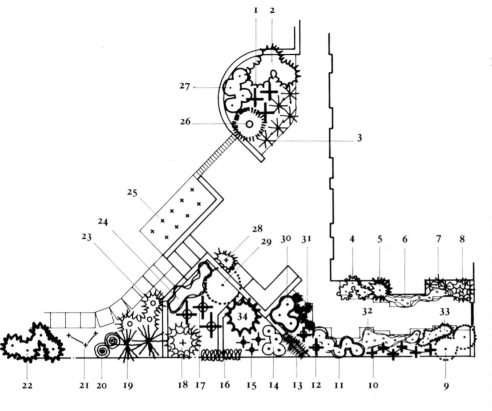

Most people have the preconceived idea that a terrace or patio must be in the back garden, close to French or sliding doors. In reality, because of the problem of shade, this may be quite impractical. If it is, I often turn the garden upside down, providing a minimal paved area close to the house to give access, and siting the main terrace in another more sheltered position, linked to the house by a path. An alternative – and it can work very well – is to use the front garden. If there is sufficient room and reasonable screening from the road, plan an extended paved area leading away from the front door. It is easy to provide the sitting area with privacy by planting that can incorporate raised beds and screening. Many people fail to realize the potential of a front garden: an area that is often large, with good access. The problem is largely psychological and the result is space not used to the full.

Position is vital, but space, too, is important and it is worth making the point that all the terraces shown here are of ample size. The space needed is directly linked to the use to which the area will be put and an estimate of this that might take into account the number of people in the family, additional space for entertaining, room for wheeled toys and for children's play, a barbecue, the possibility of a pool, planted areas and built-in seating. Many household chores can be altogether more enjoyable out of doors: an outside room as such, should be used somewhere to prepare the vegetables and do the ironing, which means that it will need power points and lighting that can be suitably insulated.

A minimum size for any terrace is in the region of 3.6 × 3.6 m (12 ft × 12 ft), not much by the time it contains a basic amount of garden furniture. If possible, make it larger: it will cost no more than a good carpet on a yard

Both these photographs show aspects of the same garden but both underline the point that patios are essentially outside rooms. Any room needs walls and here planting is used in raised beds at different levels to provide shelter and division from the further reaches of the garden

Opposite: The patio as a haven of quiet away from the hurly-burly of the outside world. The overhanging planting and the Mediterranean-style furnishings help create the illusion

by yard basis and will last considerably longer! Cheese-paring can spoil many a garden and it is a common problem. People may be more than happy to spend large amounts in and on the house, but the room outside gets forgotten or at best restricted to a minimum budget. Good materials and plants are not cheap, but you get what you pay for and most landscape products are far from over-priced. Apart from that, many plants and hard surfaces last longer than we do! That puts the whole question of value into perspective. From a purely mercenary standpoint, a well-landscaped garden and patio area always realizes more than its original price when a house is sold; in fact, in many instances it is precisely what actually sells the

house. All the gardens illustrated here would do that, which would seem to indicate that a well-planned plot is the exception rather than the rule, something I find rather disheartening.

Whatever the location – and this can vary from a tiny basement backyard to a sweep of paving with a rural view – the terrace will be the business end of entertaining and relaxing in the garden. Because it will be well used, it will need to be properly laid but before a spade goes into the ground the first consideration is the choice of materials.

In many ways we have the increase in the number of nurseries and garden centres to thank for the over-complication and fussiness of many gardens. The temptation to buy one of this and another of that leads to a jumble of pools, paving and planting that is far from restful. There is a lot of truth in the statement that the simple approach works best, whether it is applied to a set of crockery, a suit of clothes or a garden. In fact, I think that simplicity is one of the most important rules of all.

Paving materials can be broadly classified into two groups, natural and synthetic. While both can be used alongside each other in the same terrace, they have different characteristics that relate to the points mentioned at the beginning of this section: their visual potential, their practicality for a given situation and their cost.

Of the natural materials, stone is an obvious, if expensive choice. York stone is the most widely used and can be bought new or secondhand,

This is the plan of the patio shown on page 26. It uses just two materials, brick and old York stone, the former providing a visual link with the building. By turning the whole pattern at an angle to the house one creates an entirely different set of sight lines and this sets the theme for the whole garden

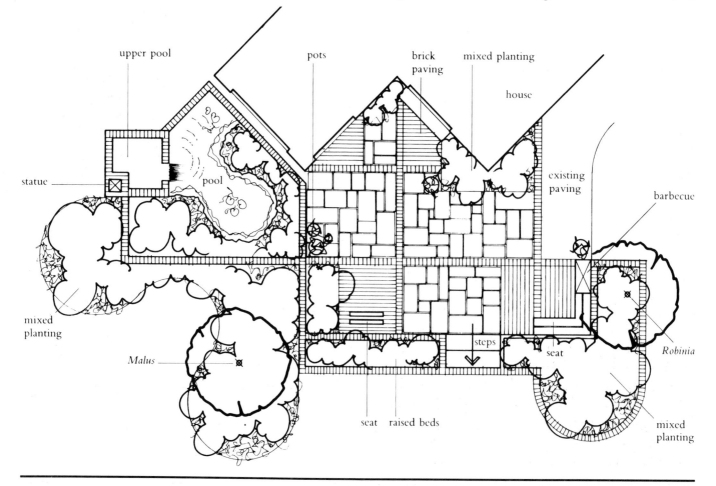

upper pool   pots   brick paving   mixed planting

house

statue

pool

existing paving

barbecue

mixed planting

Malus

steps

seat

Robinia

seat   raised beds

mixed planting

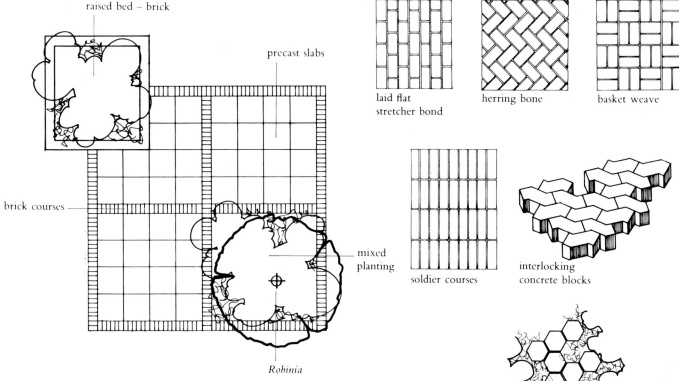

raised bed – brick

precast slabs

brick courses

mixed planting

Robinia

laid flat
stretcher bond

herring bone

basket weave

soldier courses

interlocking
concrete blocks

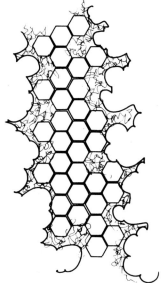

hexagonal precast slabs

broken or rectangular. Secondhand York has a charm of its own; usually from old pavements or mill floors, it is best used in random rectangular sizes that vary from massive pieces 0.9 m (3 ft) square, to small sections of about 22.5 × 22.5 cm (9 × 9 in). The thickness can range from comparatively thin slabs 2.5 cm (1 in) thick, which can be quite easily handled, to something over 10 cm (4 in). Variation can lead to difficulties in laying, for, apart from the manpower needed to carry the work out, the foundation levels will need to be adjusted. The colour of old stone can vary too, from warm, russet browns to a harder grey, often within the expanse of the terrace itself. These differences are one reason why the material is unique. It is in essense still alive, the textures reacting to light, shade and the turning seasons in a very special way.

In the gardens at the top of pages 26 and 30 random rectangular York is teamed with courses and panels of brick. In both these situations the brick does two things: it not only provides a visual link with the house but 'ties' the panels of stone into an overall pattern that joins building, steps and raised beds, thus forming an integral design. The patio on page 30 is a beautifully self-contained unit, incorporating a barbecue, built-in seating, planting at split levels – and that vital ingredient of any paved area, pots. When a high proportion of hard landscape materials is used, as in this situation, planting is essential to temper the line. The raised beds are particularly effective, foliage tumbling from level to level. As a general rule I suggest wide, generous steps, but here I used them as a 'tension point' in the design, leading feet and eye in a specific direction – the door out of this particular room.

The terrace on page 26 does something rather different. Here the whole

Brick is one of the most versatile paving materials, not only visually softening an adjoining surface but providing intimacy by its inherent small scale. Laying patterns are legion but the more complicated they are the more cutting is involved

Eating outside is one of the great pleasures of the garden. This dining area revolves around a brick barbecue and built-in seat, the raised beds and planting softening the outline

paving pattern is turned at an angle to the house and anyone leaving the building by the French windows is drawn immediately to look away on a different line to the house and boundaries, which creates a feeling of greater space. Another practical detail involves the use of a brick mowing edge along the line of the top step. This is set slightly lower than the turf, allowing the mower to run along smoothly. This eliminates that dreadful chore of hand edging: all that is needed is an annual trim with a half-moon edging iron. In a small garden this treatment, or a similar one that makes use of paving slabs, can be incorporated all round the lawn, doubling as a path and preventing damage to overhanging plants from the mower.

Broken, or crazy paving, far cheaper than cut slabs, is in many ways difficult to use close to a building. All the conflicting lines, forming an inherently 'busy' pattern, are in direct contrast to the cleaner lines of a house. One of its advantages is that it can be laid to a 'fluid' pattern, sweeping round curves and creating a feeling of space and movement. This is precisely how it has been used in the illustration on page 23. The little courtyard, with its high walls softened by planting, is laid out with a view to creating a slight air of mystery and suspense. Separate sitting areas

These two gardens provide sunny but secluded seating areas by effective use of planting and brick paving

are divided by the wing of planting that acts as a pivot to the overall design, forming another tension point with the bed on the opposite side. The upper terrace is partially screened and the highlight colours of ligularias and lilies make a telling statement against the predominantly green background.

York stone is not, of course, the only natural paving available: slabs can also be cut from slate or marble. The latter is ostentatious in the extreme, but popular for dreadful crazy paved drives in certain areas; the former has a sophisticated, cool, clear-cut line that can look superb. I can recall a basement flat in London that was floored both inside and out with riven slate, the stone being set in parallel courses that drew one out into the garden. Once outside the dark, almost black colour was sharply contrasted with white chippings and sculptural planting. The use of a similar material on both sides of French or patio doors is, of course, the strongest visual link between house and garden.

On a smaller scale, cobbles can make a useful if slightly uneven floor. They are those smooth, egg-shaped stones that are found on the beach or river bed, and like any uneven material say 'feet off'. They are useful as ideal ground cover under planting but their shapes makes them unsuitable for a sitting area.

Setts are cubes of solid granite, usually old street paving, that can look attractive used as courses to frame another paving material or to form panels and larger areas. They have a slightly uneven surface, but this can be an asset for paths or drives where grip is important.

The most popular and cost-effective paving is the precast concrete slab in all its many shapes, sizes and colours. The vast choice can create the basic problem of over-complication: all too many terraces overdo variety, particularly as far as colour is concerned. I stay well clear of anything apart from the natural sandstone colours, grey or black, the latter having a particular handsome appearance. A sensible application is shown in the little garden illustrated on page 22, where the crisp grey slabs are the perfect foil to the larger areas of brick that might otherwise become overpowering. The edge of the slabs run precisely off the edge of the raised pool, linking the two surfaces together.

One of my own favourites is the garden at the bottom of page 31. This uses a combination of brick and timber, the latter forming a bridge across a brook that adds its graceful simplicity to the charm of water. There is no need for cumbersome hand rails or florid wrought iron: just boards across the line of the garden that help to increase the visual width. Another useful device is the change of material: the brick area with its solid basketweave paving bond underlines the point that this is a sitting place, the timber indicates a change of mood and situation.

Railway sleepers can make ideal paving, as they do in the other small garden shown on the right of page 22. These solid, heavy timber beams are virtually indestructible and can be bedded on to a minimal foundation because of their weight. As in York stone, the joints between each module can be left open, forming a place for low-growing plants. (In this garden the planting again relies heavily on the shape, colour and texture of leaves rather than on flowers; the relationship between the rheum, acer and phormium is particularly telling.) Sleepers are also ideal for raised beds: laid in courses like bricks they soon mount up, but the work takes two strong men. I must admit that gardening at waist height appeals immensely to me, for why bend when plants can be brought up to a far more accessible level? Raised beds are an integral part of patio gardening as they give young plants a much-needed boost and also soften the often hard junctions between paving and walls.

So far we have looked at intrisically flat areas. The next subject is changes in level and the paths that can link these as well as different parts of the garden.

Steps can be used in many ways but, as a general rule, the wider and more generous they are, the easier they will be on both eye and feet. There is nothing more dangerous than mean steps, particularly in the winter months when there is the possibility of frost. At the top of page 31 a slight slope has been terraced into a series of gentle steps. The brick paving makes an ideal floor and the step has a slight overhang, casting a shadow

that both softens the line and gives the change of level added emphasis. The highest platform is host to a summerhouse and the planting tempers the hard line of building and paving alike. The weigela is particularly effective, helping the paving to turn that slightly awkward corner and acting as a buffer between pool and summerhouse.

The vast choice of materials available for building a terrace is available for steps too, but if the basic rules of simplicity and harmony are kept, the result will be satisfactory. Do not, for instance, suddenly change materials from, say, a brick patio to random stone steps in a quite different style. The random stone of the steps on page 32 would, however, be perfect in an informal or wild part of the garden.

In some situations steps can form the entire garden: a series of large circles or hexagons, interlocking with one another and filled with a combination of planting, grass and paving, would form a fascinating composition. In an informal situation, timber can build a fascinating flight. Railway sleepers are ideal, bedded in a random pattern that staggers its way up a slope. Soften the edge with planting so that the ends of the steps disappear into a green overhang, and end the run at a sitting area where the same material is used. Logs held in place with strong wedges would produce a similar pattern; elm is the ideal wood.

Patios *are* outside rooms: the little city courtyard on page 27 is an oasis in the heart of a city; not showy, not elaborate, just a perfect place to be on a hot summer afternoon.

Well-constructed and well-designed steps are an absolute necessity in any garden where a change of level is a problem. These examples use timber, brick and concrete in a sensible and uncluttered way

INSPIRATION FROM THE PAST

Traditional knot garden at Tryon Palace in North Carolina

In my view, historical influence has very little to do with contemporary garden design.

The development of gardens is strongly linked to sociological changes reflecting the fashion and mood of the times. It is also true to say that, until comparatively recently, gardening was almost entirely the province of the rich, although special communities – in particular the monastries and the Catholic church – have always played an important role, first in holding on to botanical knowledge in the Dark Ages and then in developing it, largely by the cultivation of plants for medicinal purposes.

It is only the last 100 years that everyman has begun to garden and it therefore follows that the art of gardening on a personal level has changed out of all proportion in that time.

However, inspiration and influence are two different matters and while the latter plays a limited role, the former opens all sorts of fascinating doors. As a working designer I am asked from time to time to either refurbish historical gardens or more occasionally to recreate them. This involves a vast amount of detailed research, including poring over old estate drawings, checking existing species to see how they deviate from the original specification and, not least, matching both hard and soft landscape materials so that the new blends imperceptibly into the old.

It could be argued that such an approach is akin to keeping a garden in deep freeze, but the matter is rather more subtle than that and centres upon the whole question of whether or not it is worth while to step back in time and as a result understand the philosophy that lay behind such individual art forms. On balance, I think it is.

Inspiration gets mixed up with awe. I am continually daunted and rather frightened by the sheer brilliance of some of the great gardens of the world. I suppose it is possible to list the real masterpieces on two hands. They would include the cascades of the Villa D'Este in Italy, the fountains of the Alhambra and the Generaliffe in Spain, the stunning but subtle arrangements of rock and sand at Kyoto in Japan, the overblown glory of Versailles and the altogether more relaxed style of Stowe or Stourhead in Britain. It is unlikely that any of these would or could be copied in any way: they are simply too good. Just occasionally people do try to emulate the Old Masters – the copy may be perfect but it inevitably lacks that spark of creation. It is, however, entirely feasible for them to inspire ideas. Dreams are never a bad thing, and these linked to observation and interpretation can increase everyone's ability. Such ability can, on occasion, lead to the creation of fresh compositions, but far more often it simply heightens our awareness of what is worth while, and that, in terms of gardening, opens up a whole new dimension.

The Knot Garden

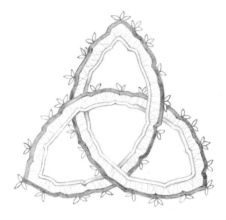

Division and edging has always been an integral part of garden design. The Romans employed stone of various patterns; later gardeners used boards, simple balustrades, smooth stones and even animal bones. As a natural progression low-growing plants became popular and the first 'knotte' is mentioned towards the end of the 15th century. The word refers to knotted cord or string that could be laid out on the ground. The spaces left between the plants or hedges were filled with a variety of materials, plants being only one of them. Bare earth was popular but needed constant attention to keep it clean. Gravel, sand, coal and chalk could each add quite different textures, while strong colour was introduced by the use of brick and tiles. Knots became an increasingly popular art form and such strong geometric shapes were best viewed from upstairs windows or higher ground, the latter often being constructed for the purpose.

Parterres extended the simple knot garden into ever more complicated patterns. Originally an Italian device, they spread across Europe, arriving in England during the 17th century. Many houses boasted enormous layouts and it is difficult to imagine the level of maintenance required to weed and tend continually what could add up to miles of hedges. The visual strength of the knot or parterre was their justification: at the time, formal bedding schemes, in which sub-tropical species were used, was unheard of. Geometry was therefore a substitute for colour, and an effective one, too.

In England very few original gardens remain from this period largely because the great landscape school of Kent, Brown and Repton destroyed

Knots are not only historical but fun, being based on endless permutations of geometric patterns. The scale can range from compositions on the grand scale to intimate modern designs that are ideal for herbs or aromatic planting

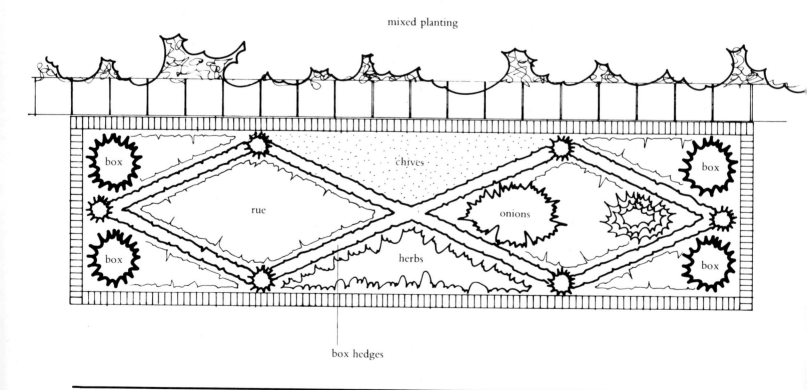

mixed planting

box

box

chives

rue

onions

box

herbs

box

box hedges

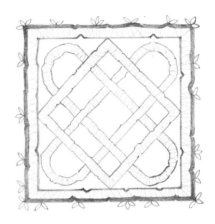

so many of them in a frenzy of 'improvement'.

Because they are labour-intensive it is hardly surprising that knots today are usually found in parks or municipal gardens, or are at least a feature of a stately home where they are able to receive constant attention. The interesting point in the majority of cases is that although the pattern of knot gardens has remained constant, the plant material used to infill that pattern has echoed horticultural development and the increasing diversity of species available. I think this is a retrograde step, on the basis of the fundamental design rule, that the simple approach is usually the most effective. It is all very well to create a complicated pattern that is visually able to stand by itself, but something quite different to dress it up with garish colour schemes that are often ill-conceived in themselves. The result all too often combines high maintenance with appalling taste: hardly sensible but an unfortunate trend in many contemporary gardens.

On a domestic level knots can be charming. They should be simple and the outline can be of clipped box, lavender or perhaps most practical of all, low brick walls. These can produce interlocking raised beds of different heights ideal for herbs which can be easily constrained.

It is interesting that two of the knots illustrated are, in fact, in America, where this style of garden flourished long after it had fallen from fashion in Europe. George Washington had a particularly fine garden in which knots and parterres are featured.

A variety of evergreen plants can be used in knots as an edging, including box and ruscus (Butcher's Broom), as these are resistant to severe winters. Dumbarton is appropriately in Washington DC and

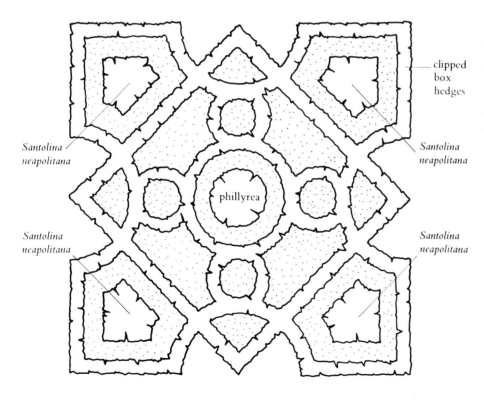

clipped box hedges

Santolina neapolitana

Santolina neapolitana

Santolina neapolitana

Santolina neapolitana

phillyrea

Box was and still is one of the best edgings for a knot. Evergreen and slow growing it has a delicious fragrance of its own that can mingle with other plants in a most delightful way. This design was taken from Gervase Markham's Countrie Farme *(1616), one of a number of books produced during the 16th and 17th centuries featuring patterns of knots and parterres*

These elaborate patterns show the knot at the zenith of its development. Cost of construction or ease of maintenance have not been an influential factor here, rather than the creation of a set piece that has enormous character in its own right. Above: Dumbarton, Washington D.C. Right: Barnsley House, Cirencester. This pattern was taken from Stephen Blake's The Compleat Gardener's Practice *(1664). The threads are all planted in box; the gold colour supplied by a golden variegated cultivar*

rather unusually uses water as a central theme (above left). Very slight changes in level are cleverly incorporated and the delicate ripples set up by the currents are echoed by the fan-shaped courses of white tiles that radiate from either end of the pattern. Scroll-shaped beds circle and intertwine round the perimeter and in summer these can be planted with annual colour to reinforce the picture. Such a complicated pattern is best contained within a simple frame, the gravel and squared trellis being sufficiently austere to act as a neutral backdrop.

Tryon Palace in North Carolina (page 34) is more traditional: clipped hedges encircling a sparkling display of spring bulbs. The hedges are also used en masse to form geometric shapes in their own right: the simple blocks of green stabilize an otherwise flamboyant picture, and white tulips also act as a foil to the brighter colour. The underlying pattern of red brick paths – which are, incidentally, perfectly laid – lead both feet and eye to the enchanting dovecot and open gate at the end of the garden.

Barnsley House in Cirencester, Gloucestershire, has a perfect knot (above). Here, low clipped box is simply infilled with gravel and this is the ideal background for such a complex pattern. The pale green leaves and grey gravel are in delicate harmony with England's soft light which is unable to stand brighter, more garish colours.

Herbs

Herbs have always been held to have a mystical quality. Long ago in prehistory they were cultivated for their culinary and medicinal powers. They still have those same attributes but in many cases their usefulness has been displaced by their ability to please the eye.

However, it is our ancesters we have to thank for the continuity that has enabled so many species to survive until the present day. Many would argue that cereals have had the greatest influence on man's development, and they are probably right, but for my money herbs run them a close second. The legends, charms, powers and potions attributed to even the most diminutive of these plants mean that they are still held in reverance by many of the world's communities.

The history of herbs is the history of the development of gardens themselves. The earliest settlements were generally circular with gardens naturally adjoining the houses. These were surrounded by agricultural land with grazing land on the outer perimeters. In the distant past, herbs, with their strong aromatic flavours and scents were a natural choice for cooking, where the quality and age of meat was often dubious. The positive flavours of herbs and their equally positive effect when eaten encouraged their use in medicine. Many herbs do indeed possess healing qualities and many are able to soothe cuts and abrasions as well as any contemporary salve. Indeed, modern drugs rely heavily on the use of herbs and associated derivatives; homoeopathy is almost entirely based on their use. Whether the placebo effect overrides any chemical ability matters not a jot: the fact is that herbs work and we need them.

During the Dark Ages monastries kept both the tradition of herb growing and plant varieties alive. Some orders, such as the Benedictines,

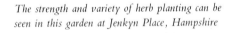

The strength and variety of herb planting can be seen in this garden at Jenkyn Place, Hampshire

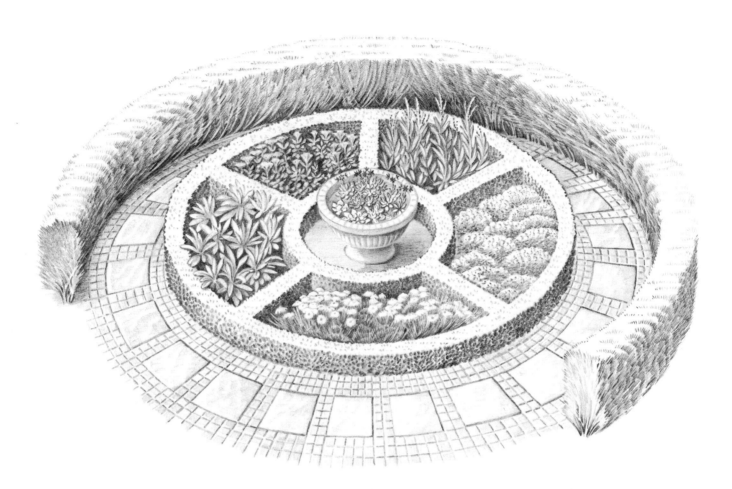

A herb wheel is traditional and in this case utilises a generous amount of room. Different species are divided by low clipped hedges and access is provided by a circular path of stone slabs and granite setts, which is echoed by the semicircular hedge in the background

were entirely vegetarian and great emphasis was placed on growing and developing new plant varieties. (Benedictine, the liqueur, is, of course, still very much alive, but the secret of the exact blend of herbs and alcohol remains a delicious secret.) As the need for inward-looking societies decreased, the use of and interest in both herbs and decorative gardening increased. Knots were often hosts to herbs while the physic garden, which was entirely devoted to their culture, was the focus of the medical world. Today only a few remain, the Chelsea Physic Garden in London being, perhaps, the most famous. It is a fascinating experience to walk through such a collection; the atmosphere must have been very different when each garden centered round a pharmacy and distillery where the essential oils were extracted by processes shrouded in mystery. It is also interesting that the Chelsea Physic Garden in particular is an enormous visual success. One moves from area to area surrounded by plants which have the most striking foliage and aromatic powers. Today we are used to gardens and virtually everyone has one.

Today there can be hardly a garden without at least one or two herbs, mint or marjoram, rosemary or sage. Ground elder, that scourge of the border, was innocently introduced by the Romans, on purely herbal grounds. It is fashionable to attribute cultural innovations to ethnic groups but ground elder is one innovation we could do without!

Although herbs are still used extensively in cooking as a flavouring rather than as a disguise, their charm is largely visual. What a variety of flower, form and foliage! We shall be looking at plantsmen's gardens a little later (see page 83) but it is the inherent interest and ease of culture that makes these plants special. In addition, virtually all of them are perennials or shrubs that either stay with us throughout the year or reappear each spring with reassuring regularity.

Because of their past, and to make gathering them for cooking easier they are usually grown as a collection. As with conifers, this is sensible because it makes it possible to see one bold pattern against another. Herbs at random, although pretty, lose some of their impact: solidarity is the order of the day.

Detail makes many a garden fascinating, and the contrasting foliage of angelica, fennel and sage sets up an interesting combination at East Lambrook, in Somerset (see page 42). Plant associations like this are worth remembering: they take a lot of the guesswork out of planning a border, which means a corresponding saving of time taken to reach maturity, often a gardener's most pressing problem.

Because of their inherent strength of line, herbs are often termed 'architectural' plants and there is no doubt that they look particularly good in close proximity to buildings, walls and hard landscape generally. I think of a stunning self-seeded rosemary that adds immeasurably to an otherwise clinical set of steps in a fine modern house and garden near Stuttgart, or of thymes creeping delicately through the joints of broken paving, or sunlight falling through fennel to cast hazy shadows.

The herb garden at Jenkyn Place in Hampshire (see page 39) is that

This is a contemporary herb garden using a series of interlocking rectangles, some at ground level, some raised. It occupies a small area and would be ideal in a limited space

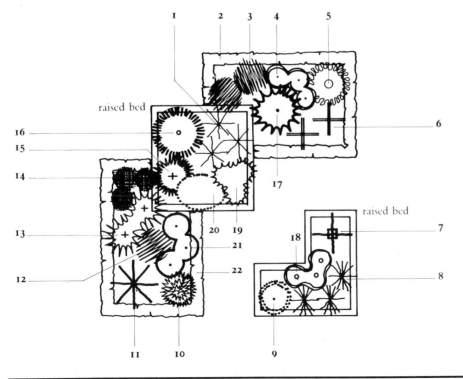

Key to planting plan

1	common sage
2	chives as border
3	purple sage
4	bush basil
5	lavender
6	hyssop
7	vervain
8	golden marjoram
9	clove carnations
10	oregano
11	common thyme
12	white hybrid tea rose
13	rue
14	chamomile
15	sweet cicely
16	French marjoram
17	white hybrid tea rose
18	violets
19	sorrel
20	tarragon
21	annual clary sage
22	cotton lavender

Above and right: *The joy of herbs is not just their smell and culinary qualities but also their good looks. There can be few groups of plants with such character and underlying quality of form and style. Use them to good effect wherever you can*

typical English compromise between order and chaos, but is has undeniable charm. The focus of the garden is a starkly white figure that would have been far too dull in a more conventional sandstone. Old flag paths radiate from this point, plants growing through and tumbling over the slabs. Golden marjoram, ornamental onions, fennel and comfrey have all combined to produce a strongly modelled picture that is tempered by the soft grey artemesia.

A final and more traditional herb garden lies within the gardens at Barnsley House in Gloucestershire (above). Here, a collection is contained within a geometric arrangement of box hedges, in themselves an aromatic frame. This certainly has an historical link with a true knot, but where the latter was almost inevitably severe, this one is tempered by a riot of foliage, the underlying clipped hedges barely keeping control. This is a purely English garden and underlines the telling fact that herbs are astonishingly easy to grow – something that assures their success in a maintenance-conscious gardening society.

Victorian Bedding

The 19th century in England saw not only the success of the Industrial Revolution but a complete upheaval in the world of gardening. Gone were the sublime landscape parks of William Kent and 'Capability' Brown whose existence continued for a time under the direction of Humphrey Repton. Gone, too, was the basic premise that gardens were the preserve solely of the wealthy. At last the doors were flung open – or, at least, the merchant and middle classes were able to own their own park in miniature, which usually consisted of a scaled-down vision of the acres their grandfathers knew, complete with serpentine pools, meandering paths and a fondness for rustic work in the shape of summerhouses and gazebos.

What brought about this obsession for detail was a huge increase in house building and a corresponding reduction in the size of gardens. The ubiquitous villa reigned supreme and the beginnings of what we now

The Fernery at Southport Botanic Garden uses a riot of foliage that is redolent of those Victorian follies and grottoes that lingered on in the 19th century

This pot is planted with various types of pelargonium, a typical Victorian bedding plant

term suburban sprawl was becoming a reality. In other words, gardening and the supply of every conceivable species of plant suddenly became big business. This was due in great measure to the plant collectors, some famous, others less well known, who searched the world from the Himalayas to South Africa and the Far East. Such men as Joseph Hooker, Sir Joseph Banks, Thunberg, E. H. Wilson and Charles Sargent have all given their names to plants, not just in Britain but in other parts of the world as well. With this mania for collection came an increasing preoccupation with colour, a trend which really became established in the latter part of the 19th century, at the height of Queen Victoria's reign. Low-growing introductions from sub-tropical parts of the world were used and a far greater range of species than carried by any nursery today could be seen in most gardens. The majority of these plants were half-hardy, or tender perennials, and the earliest of them, introduced about 1835, included verbena and pelargoniums. Fortunately, this date coincided with the great development of conservatories and greenhouses, where stock plants could be overwintered to supply the next season's display.

Whether the results of such labour could be called an indigenous style is open to debate, but colourful it most certainly was. Vibrant reds, yellows and oranges sprang out from beds usually set out in a geometric pattern that added to the visual confusion. As if colour was not enough, the Victorian preoccupation with ornaments meant that many beds had a centrepiece of some kind. Urns, rustic pillars and bowls brought the third dimension into play, and gushed with flowers.

Today very little of this work is carried on, mainly because propogation, planting and maintenance would run up a bill of astronomic proportions. Some local authorities, particularly at the seaside where growing conditions are more favourable, continue the trend, and a few stately homes have the labour and cash available for public displays. On a domestic scale, bedding is generally used as a filler between shrubs and hardy perennials, sown or planted out in drifts that produce a rather more restful picture.

However, not all bedding was of the carpet variety, a term referring to the geometric patterns found in rugs and copied so enthusiastically by the Victorians. There was also a certain predeliction for gloom and the creation of sombre collections of ferns and similar species. Sometimes great sections of parks were planted with palms, grasses, monsteras and ferns, set in dells and among dripping rocks that added atmosphere to the composition. Here, too, could be found those curious clinker walls, so popular at the time and still occasionally unearthed in domestic gardens. Botanic gardens often maintain the tradition and the Fernery at Southport in the north-west of England houses a fine collection in a setting that belongs to the past of a century ago (see page 43).

Again, cost put an end to most of these displays but fashion was such that hardy species such as bamboo, laurel, fatsia and aucuba outlasted them on a more permanent basis.

Labour was the key to the Victorian garden and although as many machines as new plants were devised to ease this problem, the variety of features were directly related to manpower. In terms of sheer hard work, rockeries were difficult to beat, the earliest being built about the turn of the 19th century. At first they were simply random heaps of stone, a form that is still all too common today. It was not until the 1850s, when a genuine interest was taken in alpines, that rock was set in a natural fashion. Some of the more bizzarre gardens actually went out of their way to recreate specific locations. Perhaps the best known of these was at Friar Park in Berkshire where the Matterhorn and surrounding region was built with something approaching 10,000 tons of rock, complete with artificial snow and livestock. The individual rocks were not small: a number weighed 10,000 kg (10 tons), and to use them without modern earthmoving eqqipment and cranes was no mean achievement.

So, whether the Victorians are remembered for their obsession with colour and detail, their crusades across the globe in search of exotic plants or their genius for invention, there is no doubt that within the space of 80 years or so, they changed the face of the gardening world. Many of those changes are still with us today and whether the results are loved or hated, the tenacity that went into creating them is something to admire.

Above and right: *Victorian bedding relied heavily on the use of tender and half hardy plants to create vivid and often garish displays. While such a style has a place in seaside parks it is hardly relevant to today's domestic garden where maintenance is often a major consideration However, a brilliant effect can be obtained using a careful selection of woody and perennial plants with favourite bedding subjects*

Cottage Gardens

To many garden historians the great parks of the mid–18th century were the only native British landscape style. To my mind, they may be sublime, but they swept away much of the earlier traditions that had developed over a far longer time.

Evolving in their own individual and unspectacular way were cottage gardens. Theirs is a style that is fluid, has few ground rules and relies very heavily on the personality of the owner. Since cottage gardening is very much alive today, here is an art form that spans a far longer time than almost any other horticultural fashion.

Like most styles, cottage gardening was born of need in an age when a home-owner had to be self-sufficient. It was not an urban phenomenon because town dwellers have always had services and supplies to support them. A cottage garden at one time had to maintain vegetables, fruit, herbs, beehives, cut flowers, and possibly livestock in the form of chickens and a goat; today the pressure is off food production and on visual qualities that complement both house and surrounding rural setting. The old criterion still works best, precisely because it *is* a productive environment, one area or section positively relating to, and dependent upon, another. The old methods centered round a rotational crop system and the garden was continually on the move. This meant a healthy vegetable and flower garden, both being kept in heart by liberal applications of organic material. It is a fact that although our modern lifestyle has brought about

Below and bottom: *Traditional thatched cottages and their equally traditional planting and gardens*

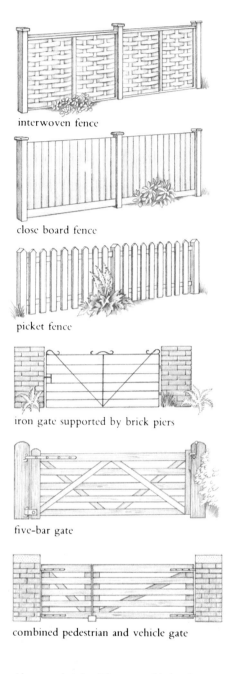

interwoven fence

close board fence

picket fence

iron gate supported by brick piers

five-bar gate

combined pedestrian and vehicle gate

great advances in the standard of living it has also reduced the need for the old-style cottage garden. This has been hastened by the advance of suburbia and the inevitable scramble by well-heeled city dwellers for a house in the country. Such people undoubtably rescue many fine buildings from dereliction, but they naturally bring a whole new set of values with them. The set piece, 'chocolate box' type of modern cottage garden, with an idealized thatched cottage and pristine picket fences, may be pretty but never has that slightly untidy or semi-chaotic urgency of its ancestors.

There are, nevertheless, some exceptionally attractive gardens still to be seen in most parts of Britain. One feature of a cottage garden is the emphasis often put on the front approach and on the use of climbing plants on the building. Look at the fine old thatch on page 47. An area has been extended by the door, solid brick piers supporting overhead beams that are smothered in a combination of wisteria and roses. The climbers have been allowed to run riot, going up the straw roof and extending the link between house and garden. Many people feel concern about the possible damage to roofs and brickwork done by such plants, but as long as the tendrils are prevented from working their way between slates or tiles, or actually through the eaves, there should be no problem.

Gravel is traditionally a rural material; it is cheap, can conform to a curving pattern and, because of its colour, is able to blend visually with brick and stone alike. The garden on page 47 uses it and so, too, does the delightful composition at the bottom of the same page. At a glance all this planting looks quite random, but in fact nothing could be further from the truth. For a start the old pear tree – and it is a beauty – acts as a pivot for the underlying bed and a frame for the cottage in the background. Plants include day liles, phlox, foxgloves and the striking evergreen leaves of the greater periwinkle. The silver foliaged senecis acts as a carpet at the front of the border and the classic combination of grey and purple is linked across the simple gravel path by *Berberis thunbergii* 'Atropurpurea'. The access to the lawn is quite narrow, all wrong for a modern architectural garden but just right in this intimate setting. Another part of the same

Above and right: The nuts and bolts of any garden are particularly important and this is nowhere more apparent than in the careful choice of gates and boundaries. Respect local styles and traditions wherever possible

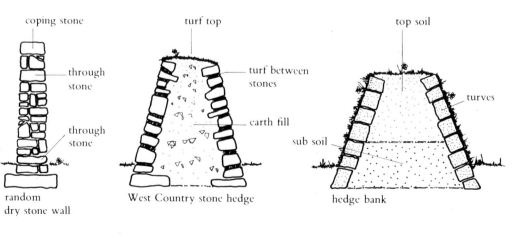

coping stone

through stone

through stone

random dry stone wall

turf top

turf between stones

earth fill

West Country stone hedge

top soil

turves

sub soil

hedge bank

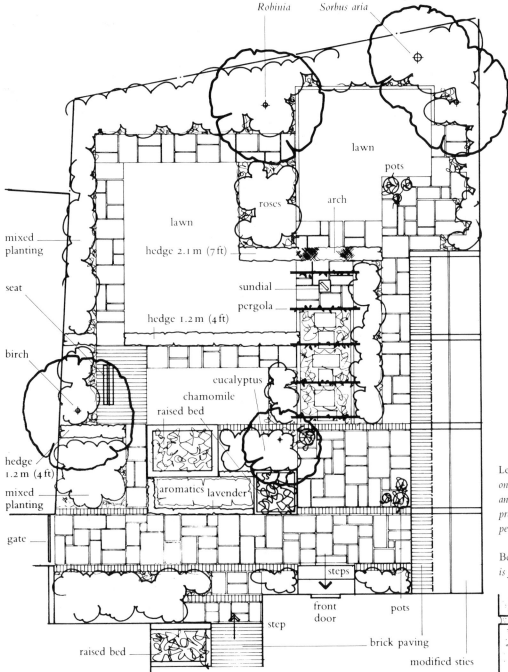

Robinia *Sorbus aria*

lawn

pots

roses

arch

lawn

mixed
planting

hedge 2.1 m (7 ft)

seat

sundial

pergola

hedge 1.2 m (4 ft)

birch

eucalyptus

chamomile
raised bed

hedge
1.2 m (4 ft)

mixed
planting

aromatics lavender

gate

steps

front
door

pots

step

raised bed

brick paving

modified sties

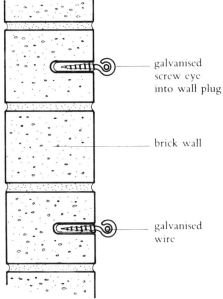

Left: *This is a modern cottage garden that relies on traditional materials. Old York stone, brick and planting combine to form a restful but practical design that revolves around the central pergola*

Below: *Using wires on walls to accept climbers is far more practical than erecting yards of trellis*

galvanised
screw eye
into wall plug

brick wall

galvanised
wire

garden is shown on the opposite page, the unpretentious timber seat fitting comfortably against the old stone wall. Fruit trees form a backdrop and this little corner is full of colour, with some of my favourite cottage plants, such as aquilegia, anthirrhinums and alchemilla playing a prominent role. In fact, this is the sort of setting where the introduction of a few vegetables, or at least salad crops, would not go amiss: lettuce, courgettes, with those magnificent leaves and rather untidy habit, and the king of border crops, globe artichokes. The blue of their flower heads is marvellous, the equal of that of any hybridized plant. Just visible in the illustration is the gravel path leading to the seat, and it is the use of this unobtrusive surface that gives continuity to the whole garden. The gravel

The planting of cottage gardens should always respect the surrounding rural environment, using wherever possible a fair proportion of wild flowers. The gravel paths and stone walls shown here respect local building materials, adding to the charm of the garden

is also indigenous to the area, and has a natural link with the stone wall.

Walls can make or mar a composition: the modern tendency to use wide mortar joints that squash out like toothpaste may be cheaper but looks hideous. Dry stone walls are best of all in a rural setting but usually need a craftsman to build them, to grade the sizes and incorporate 'through' stones to tie the wall together. Another problem with walls are climbers, or, rather, the provision of proper support for them. All too often this is a jumble of string and wire, held together with rusty nails. Trellis is a somewhat better alternative, but too dominant, detracting from the beauty of the plant. Horizontal wires, stretched between vine eyes or masonry nails are ideal. They can be spaced at 60 cm (2 ft) intervals up the wall and it is simple enough to tie a plant to them. They are, in addition, virtually invisible.

Wander down the path in the garden illustrated above. It is early summer: foxgloves, poppies and roses are in bloom and there are traditional ground cover plants, such as epimedium and hosta. A more nostalgic or traditional picture would be hard to find.

Gertrude Jekyll

Gertrude Jekyll was born in 1843 and died 89 years later, in 1932. Her lifetime spanned an age of vast change, from the Victorian era to comparatively recent times. The revolution she brought about in gardening has had an equally powerful impact on the horticultural world.

During her childhood, spent at Bramley in Surrey, she gained a love of both buildings and the wildlife of a country area, and expressed this at first in painting. She was certainly influenced by the Impressionist School and may well have strengthened her appreciation of colour harmonies by studying Chevreul's colour wheel, which had been published in 1839.

Although she is best known for her conception and superb planning of flower borders, Gertrude Jekyll also had an acute eye for the management of altogether larger areas, woodland and water playing an important part. At Munstead Wood in Surrey, her own garden, she graded borders into a backdrop of trees, avoiding a sharp transition and relying heavily on subtle colour changes.

She was influenced, too, by contemporaries. Her early friendship with William Robinson was particularly fruitful, reinforcing her use and understanding of hardy perennials, the backbone of much of her planting. Robinson was a great advocate of natural species and associations and this

Above and below: *Throughout Getrude Jekyll's gardens runs the underlying theme of Lutyens's superb architecture. Brick paving and balustrade in both illustrations underline the point; also good planting is the perfect foil to fine buildings*

was the key to Gertrude Jekyll's work. She always recommended planting material that would thrive in a specific situation, whether it be a hot sunny bank or a cool moist border. This view is in direct contrast to that of many garden architects, both then and now, who are often more concerned with striking plant relationships than with growing conditions. Any sensible plantsman or designer knows that the first is impossible without the second.

As Gertrude Jekyll was inspired by her contemporaries, so has she in turn influenced designers following her. All too often the effect of looking back over one's shoulder to emulate a past style is counterproductive, but not as far as Miss Jekyll's particular magic is concerned. Perhaps the secret lies in the characteristics of the plant material itself. Even if a scheme is faithfully reproduced it is bound to take on not only the slight variations in the initial positioning of material but will react to the microclimate and other local conditions. This makes a different composition each time and in addition keeps the whole concept fresh.

It was in 1891 that Gertrude Jekyll met the great architect, Edwin Lutyens, who was at the time unknown. For the next 50 years she maintained their association and collaborated with Lutyens on many gardens. For many people, myself among them, Lutyens' architecture brought the English country house to its climax. His sense of line, like that of all the best architects, did not stop at the building, but extended to a series of sweeping terraces, steps and lawns that formed a natural link between house and garden. Gertrude Jekyll breathed life into what were superb geometric patterns and over the years displayed an astonishing grasp of what today would be called landscape architecture.

In 1908 she worked at Hestercombe, and although many of her schemes have faded or been replaced, this garden in Somerset has been recreated, keeping to the original planting plans as faithfully as possible. The picture at the top of page 51 shows a typical example of Lutyens' fine stonework. Thin courses are capped by a finely detailed balustrade flanking a broad flight of steps. In a typically bold statement, the yucca pinpoints the end of the balustrade, taking the eye down to the less formal planting below. Blue and white were one of Gertrude Jekyll's favourite combinations and in her book, *Colour Schemes for the Flower Garden*, she says, 'For instance a blue garden, for beauty's sake, may be hungering for a group of white lilies, or something of palest lemon yellow, but is not allowed to have it.' She is talking about the purist attitude towards planting design: purists can be dangerous people and Gertrude Jekyll, for all her sensitivity and perception, was fortunately never one of them. In the corner of Hestercombe in the illustration, the delphineums and regal lilies use the same blue and white combination, with the grey below creating a perfectly blended triangle.

On page 53 are reproduced a section and the layout of a chapter on 'special colouring' from Jekyll's book *Colour Schemes for the Flower Garden*. The total length of this layout is something approaching 120 m (400 ft) and the gold garden is stunning. The scale ranges from golden planes at the back, through elaeagnus and privet, down to box and euonymus at the lowest level. And Miss Jekyll was not averse to using annuals: the primrose-coloured african marigolds and snapdragons are delightful. A sundial forms the centrepiece of the walk and Gertrude Jekyll's instructions stated firmly that the letters should not be gilded: the colour would be quite wrong.

In direct contrast is Gertrude Jekyll's use of hot colours at Barrington Court in Somerset (see bottom of page 51). Red, yellow and orange are again tempered by grey. This underlines her concept of using colour in tonal ranges, a technique that increases the visual harmony – and, incidentally, the size of a garden – while reinforcing continuity.

It is an old truth that there is nothing new in design, but Gertrude Jekyll brought a unique freshness to the subject.

Although Miss Jekyll was something of a purist she never allowed this approach to dominate her sensitive style. Within any composition, even within a single colour, there was great diversity of form and foliage, not to mention interest throughout the year

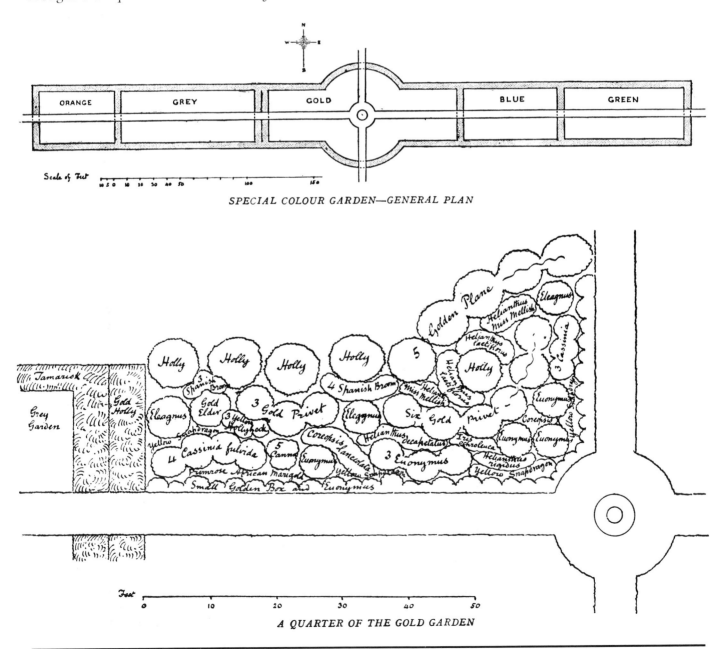

SPECIAL COLOUR GARDEN—GENERAL PLAN

A QUARTER OF THE GOLD GARDEN

WATER
AND ITS INFLUENCE

In Britain, with its temperate, maritime climate, water in all its forms plays a dominant role. A mist of rain softening the landscape, a stream or river, the still reflections on a lake, or a wild sea, are all part of the British awareness.

Where water is plentiful it is taken for granted but in other parts of the world it is seen as what it is: vital to life and to the survival of communities. For this reason it takes on an importance that the West cannot always understand and has always played a significant part in the garden of hot, dry countries. A garden such as the Court of Myrtles at Alhambra, in Spain, for example, is an expression of the sheer delight of moving water surrounded by brilliant white, sun-drenched walls; just as pleasing are the reflections in that great canal in front of the Taj Mahal. These may be grand compositions, but they underline man's desire to use and celebrate his most vital natural resource.

In lands less dependent on rainfall, the way in which water is used as a decorative element changes. The landscape designers of the 18th century dammed streams to form lakes and created changes of level to produce waterfalls, and both imitated rather than formed a sharp contrast to a natural background. Later styles reduced the scale of such features but retained the informality, often to the detriment of a garden's layout in visual terms. Today, because of the ever-decreasing size of plots, water is often relegated to ponds and pools so small that it is difficult to maintain a balanced environment within them. Nevertheless, water gardening is big business and expanding. A visit to a garden centre or nursery shows the vast selection of prefabricated ponds, liners, pumps and equipment, not to mention fish and plants.

The attraction is an obvious one: the sight – and, more importantly, the sound – of water on a hot summer afternoon is irresistible. On a slightly deeper plane, particularly in an urban situation, there is still that basic psychological desire to turn one's back on a hostile city. In essence it is escapism and the use of water in all its guises is one of the best ways of achieving this. It is a great pity, therefore, that so many gardens are spoilt by poorly thought out and designed water features of one kind or another. This is almost invariably because of the vast range of options available. Should a pool be formal or informal? What depth should it be to support pond life? Would a rockery be in keeping with it? Consider the delights of a bog garden with the wealth of species such conditions demand. Consider the possibilities of a mill stone fountain, water bubbling and sliding over a riven surface to drop into a bed of smooth cobbles. This section looks at all these possibilities underlining again the point that simplicity and respect for materials are the key to good design.

Pools

I always find the word pool misleading, or if not that, then vague. It is really a generic term for formal and informal arrangements of every conceivable shape, size and pattern, geometric or otherwise. The main criterion is, of course, that it contain a reasonable area of relatively still water: too large and it becomes a lake, too fast and it turns into a stream or cascade.

The best pools – and all those illustrated here are excellent examples of the art of pool making – reflect a theme, and this harks back to a basic rule of garden design. Broadly interpreted it is that areas close to a house should be architectural, to make a positive link with the building, while the further away they are, the softer and looser a composition becomes. When this is translated into pool design, it makes sense that an area of water can blend into a crisply detailed terrace or patio if the overall lines of paving, steps and hard landscape generally are respected. Unfortunately, the opposite is often the case: a pool of serpentine shape is totally unrelated

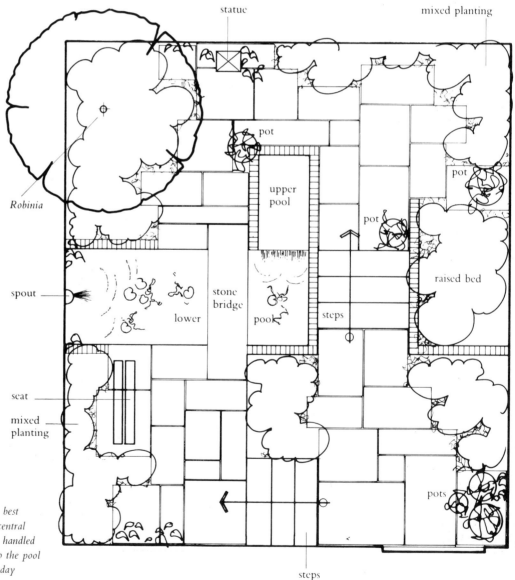

This town-house courtyard is the very best outdoor room, with water acting as a central theme. The change of level is sensibly handled while the sound of water dropping into the pool would be delightful on a hot summers day

to its surroundings. It not only looks uncomfortable but is normally difficult to build as paving has to be laboriously cut in round the edges.

If you look upon the garden as a reflection of your own personality then the individual elements within it are equally important. Do not get carried away by the garish commercialism of garden centres or you will live to regret it. Choose a design that is right for you and that will stand the test of time once the initial enthusiasm has worn off.

A classically designed pool is shown at the top left on page 59. The whole layout has been built on an underlying grid and the brief was to create a formal garden, using relatively inexpensive modern materials, where maintenance could be kept to a minimum. The hard landscape uses only two basic surfaces, concrete block paviors, easily laid on a bed of compacted sand, and washed pea gravel. The pool acts as a unifying element, running up the centre of the garden and leading the eye to a simple but beautifully constructed seat. The courses of paviors act as the

Key to planting plan

1	2	*Arundinaria nitida*
2	3	*Hydrangea serrata* 'Greyswood'
3	1	*Hydrangea petiolaris*
4	2	*Hydrangea macrophylla* 'Blue Wave'
5	2	*Arundinaria viridistriata*
6	1	*Hedera helix* 'Gold Heart'
7	1	*Rheum palmatum*
8	2	*Euphorbia griffithii* 'Fireglow'
9	1	*Parthenocissus henryana*
10	2	*Phlomis fruticosa*
11	1	*Cistus* × *purpureus*
12	1	*Mahonia lomariifolia*
13	2	*Anemone japonica* (white)
14	1	*Actinidia kolomikta*
15	1	*Wisteria sinensis*
16	2	*Choisya ternata*
17	3	*Acanthus spinosa*
18	1	*Jasminum officinale*
19	1	*Fatsia japonica*
20	1	*Clematis tangutica*
21	1	*Philadelphus coronarius* 'Variegatus'
22	5	*Epimedium sulphureum*
23	4	*Alchemilla mollis*
24	4	*Hebe pinguifolia* 'Pagei'
25	1	*Rosmarinus officinalis* 'Miss Jessop's Upright'
26	5	*Festuca glauca*
27	2	*Potentilla* 'Tilford Cream'
28	3	*Hosta* 'Frances Williams'
29	3	*Hyssopus aristatus*
30	3	*Hebe subalpina*
31	1	*Euphorbia wulfenii*
32	3	*Hosta* 'Thomas Hogg'
33	3	*Potentilla* 'Red Ace'
34	5	*Festuca scoparius*
35	2	*Cytisus* × *kewensis*
36	2	*Viburnum davidii*
37	6	*Skimmia japonia* 'Rubella'

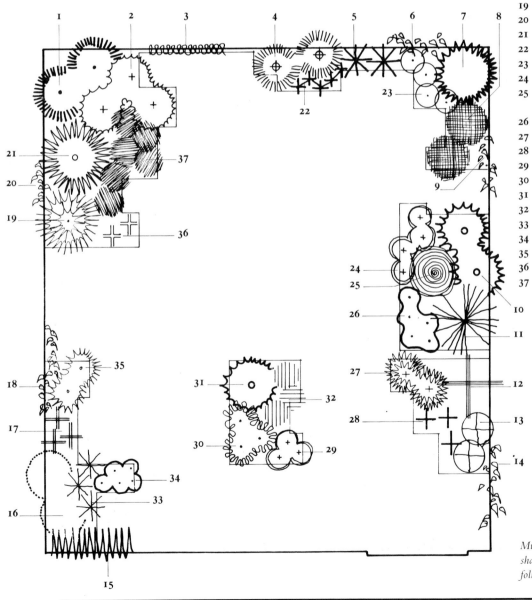

Much courtyard planting has to be tolerant of shade. Such plants often compensate with bold foliage and year-round interest

Above and below: *Two original water features – a fountain and a pond (the pond is a detail of the garden shown on page 54)*

grid, positively tying the features together and preventing either of the surfaces from becoming too dominant. It is a matter of aesthetics always to ensure that the pool sides and bottom are black, either painted concrete or black butyl rubber. This has the effect of giving the water added depth, because it is difficult to see the bottom at all. Levels around a pool are extremely important: if they are untrue, the water appears to be running at an angle, which is both impossible and a visual disaster! In the illustration the job has been carried out by craftsmen, the coping just overhanging the water, casting a gentle shadow that softens the line between the two mediums. I am very fond of using stepping stones: they not only lead both the eye and feet in a particular direction, but when they are in water give a real feeling of involvement, a heightening of the senses. It is essential that the slabs, or whatever material is being used, are large enough. It is all to easy to put a foot wrong – literally – with disastrous consequences! The slabs in the illustrated pool are built of solid brick piers at a height that makes it seem that they are floating on the surface of the water.

The long bed at the back of the garden has been raised, giving young plants a boost and softening the line of the concrete block wall, itself a handsome feature when well laid and set off with a coping of paviors that form a link with the floor.

Both these gardens are strongly architectural and use water as a central theme. Coupled to this is the use of planting that softens the crisp line of walls and paving, tying the various elements together

The garden above is formal, and so, too, is that shown on page 54, but here the setting is more intimate: a tiny town garden, floored in well-laid old York stone and surrounded by walls draped in greenery. The slight changes in level have been used with skill, the pool and paving dropping from one height to another. This same garden is shown at the top of page 58 where the lower angle shows the simple but effective stone bridge. Such a strong line brings the figure into focus, the latter acting as a foil to the essentially evergreen background. Statues, busts, pots and any other kind of focal point must always have a specific place. It is not unusual to see a fine piece slapped down anywhere, doing justice neither to itself nor to the garden composition as a whole. The more architectural a statue is, the better it looks in association with plants, and in this case the figure is surrounded by the bold leaves of fatsia, phormium and the potted palm.

The pool has movement too, the water sliding over a stone sill to be recirculated by a submersible pump. Not only does this create visual interest and sound but it helps to aerate the water, important in a small pond stocked with fish. The bottom pool of a system should always be at least twice as big as the top one, otherwise, when water is pumped round the circuit, the lowest pool rapidly empties!

People often ask whether a pool is better constructed in concrete or with some kind of plastic liner. Until relatively recently, concrete was the only material, and although pools could be made quite readily, the amount of physical work involved was considerable. This included

This is the plan of the garden shown on the left of page 59 and underlines the point that geometry can form the basis of excellent garden design. Water plays a dominant role acting as a spine between the two asymmetric patterns to either side

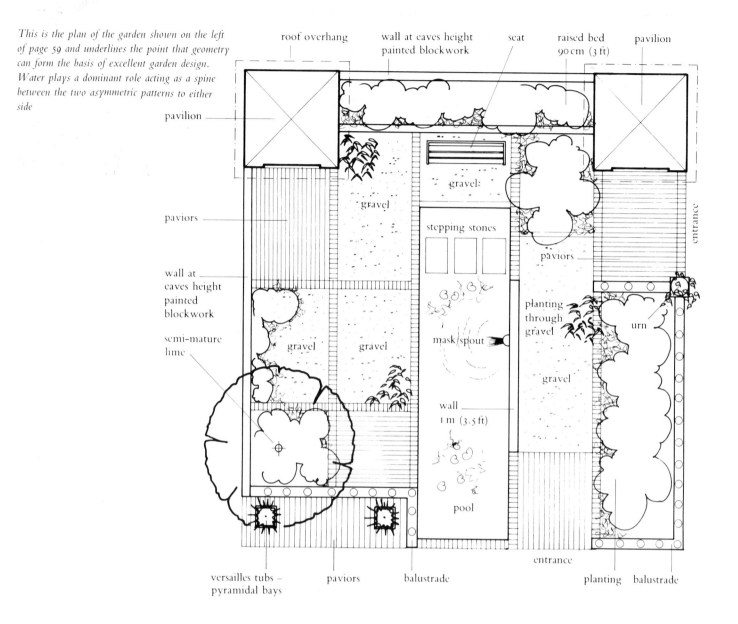

digging out, placing hardcore, constructing timber shuttering, pouring concrete and ensuring adequate reinforcement. Finally the pool had to be rendered and every effort made to eliminate the lime which works out of the cement. In addition, there was the ever-present risk of the appearance of hairline cracks, which are almost impossible to locate. The conclusion is pretty obvious: use a liner. Liners come in various grades, of which butyl rubber is the strongest. They are easy to fit, relatively cheap and last a very long time. They have their drawbacks, like anything else, being susceptible to small boys with bows and arrows, and tending to pucker up in the corners when made to conform to a rectangular shape. The latter problem can usually be kept to a minimum, being, in any case, below water level, while a puncture repair kit looks after the former. The problem is not so much the making good, as the arduous task of removing what is left of the water, fish and plants.

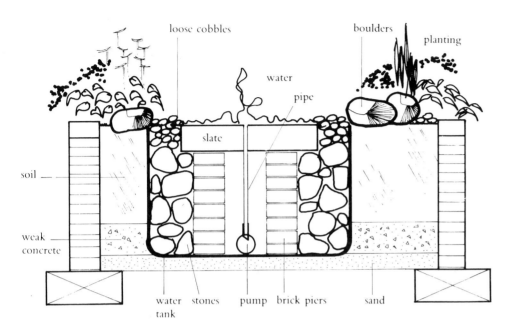

loose cobbles

boulders

planting

water

pipe

slate

soil

weak
concrete

water
tank

stones

pump

brick piers

sand

Left: *Not all water need take the shape of pools. Here a piece of slate has been set within a water tank. Water is pumped through the stone and slides back into the tank in a continuous cycle. Such a feature is very safe where young children are present*

Below: *Overlapping timber decks jut out into a large pool or lake. Such a feature could be a well-detailed landing stage or an unusual sitting area; in both instances it has a slightly Japanese influence*

All these elements make up a balanced pool environment. Both plants and fish are necessary, for one without the other disrupts the oxygen balance and turns the pool green, a common sight. Do not confuse this with the inevitable greening over of a new pool which always happens until the inhabitants have settled down. Too small a water area also does this and I always stipulate a minimum size 1.8 × 1.8 m (6 × 6 ft) or a multiple of these dimensions.

Both pools on page 59 use butyl liners, carried up behind the brickwork in the right-hand photograph so that it is invisible. Here, again, there is skillful use of a change of level, the lawn and planting descending in a series of terraces and raised beds. The planting is particularly fine, the bronze Japanese maple blending with the warm coloured brick. Waterside species include the yellow-flowered trollius, rogersia and that old favourite, hostas. The top of the pool acts as a mowing edge to the

Beth Chatto's garden is a lesson in controlled planting design. Water plays an important role, moisture tolerant species merging into lawns and finally the taller backdrop of trees

lawn, the turf being set at a slightly higher level.

Bricks and mortar are not the only construction materials: railway sleepers have been brilliantly incorporated in the garden shown at the bottom of the page. These were used as paving in the patio section (opposite) but here they are stacked up to retain the garden alongside this small canal. In the middle of the garden a stream has been channelled between sleepers turned in the other direction, bolted together and treated with pitch to keep them watertight. Not only does this feature have enormous physical strength, it possesses visual power as well and such positive lines need equally positive planting. The rheum to one side and the ferns to the other are just right. There is virtually no flower colour here at all, apart from the sweep of cream astilbes in the background, and this heightens the drama. Colour is used far too often to compensate for poor design, and this arrangement stands the test without faltering.

Sometimes a garden is simply too small for a pool, or the presence of young children may make the introduction of water undesirable. One way round this is to create some sort of feature that uses water but in a minimal quantity. The design illustrated at the top of page 61 uses a millstone, or a slab of slate, granite or marble or even a smooth, round boulder. This feature is drilled through the middle, and water is pumped up, through the hole to slide over the surface and return to the sump beneath. Prefabricated millstone fountains are available but lack character. The best solution is a visit to a stone mason (or a scrap yard) to find the piece you want; it will be unique and it will suit your personality, two essentials for any garden feature.

Bold foliage is always the perfect foil to a sheet
of water. The circular lily pads float like rafts in
the illustration above while the great leaves of
Rheum palmatum *have the strength to temper
the strong visual line created by the railway
sleepers in the picture on the left*

*A watermill is sheer escapism and this example
was built for and displayed at the 1985
Chelsea Flower Show. It utilises traditional
construction with superb planting, the water
being recirculated by a powerful submersible pump*

Construction is relatively simple, and the illustration suggests using a
raised bed as a host. In this way the feature not only doubles as a seat but
comes closer to eye and hand level; children in particular will find it
fascinating. The whole unit is housed within a water tank, of the kind
found in lofts. This is carefully positioned so that the top of the tank is just
below the coping of the surrounding walls. Brick piers are built in the
position shown and the millstone or slab placed squarely on top of these. A
submersible pump is positioned at the bottom, between the piers, and
connected to a pipe that runs up and through the centre hole of the stone.
Large stones are placed round the piers, and these are topped with loose
cobbles that can be allowed to spill out over the adjoining planted area,
disguising the lip of the water tank. When the tank is filled and the pump
activated, water flows round the system in a continuous cycle, needing
only an occasional top-up to compensate for evaporation.

I once built this arrangement in the garden of a bee-keeper. The pump
was turned down to produce a minimal flow so that the level of the water
running over the stone was reduced to a trickle. Bees are thirsty creatures
and on a hot summer there was a constant procession of hundreds of these
insects alighting to drink, a really remarkable sight.

One other aspect of the technical side of water gardening is lighting. As
with most things, moderation is likely to bring success and the well-placed
floodlight or spot can bring a pool alive in a way that daylight cannot.
This is largely due to the dramatic effect of the surrounding darkness, the

water being thrown into sharp relief. Underwater lights are obtainable, specially sealed and totally safe. Sometimes these can be successful, if they are used in moderation and give a plain white light. To be avoided at all costs are the floating, rotating halographic nightmares that create an atmosphere like that of a fairground or a seaside resort (like Blackpool) at the height of the season. White and blue light, set inconspicuously in a neighbouring planted area, is all that is needed; red, green, and orange are to be avoided, they turn foliage a revolting colour that detracts from rather than enhances the setting.

Beth Chatto is one of Britain's most famous gardeners, a real plantswoman whose work is discussed in another part of this book (see page 88). The illustration on page 62 shows a section of her water garden and no one could ask for a better or more finely composed picture. It is all here: the sensibly detailed bank, held in check by elm boards and wedges, the lawn sweeping away to a backdrop of largely evergreen planting, and the more intimate waterside species, culminating in the great leaves of *Gunnera manicata*. Not a plant for the fainthearted, this: a massive hardy perennial that likes to dangle its toes in a moist boggy spot. It dies down completely in the winter, the crowns being covered with the old leaves, then erupts into life again in the spring with great spikes of strange ruddy flower. Each leaf can be over 1.8 m (6 ft) across, so this is not a plant for the small garden, but in the right situation it is unforgettable.

This pool is natural, no liners or concrete here; it uses most the traditional method of puddled clay. With the basic ingredients of low ground and running water, a little ingenuity and a lot of hard work does the rest and is well worth it.

Scale is an important element in garden design and while Beth Chatto has the room to paint an expansive picture, many people have to be satisfied with rather less space. In the tiny, gem-like pool at the bottom of page 58, there is no space for aquatic plants or fish, and no need for it. The circular pattern turns in upon itself, its focus the delightful fountain rose. Arms outstretched in the best Hollywood style, the ring of figures clutch at the soaring spray that falls back to ripple the water gently. Old paving surrounds the pool, small cobbles filling the joints between the stone slabs. Planting reinforces the pattern, the ferns providing just the right note of informality, the delicate purple violas acting as a subtle foil.

To have a balanced environment, a pool must contain plants and fish. Of course, these are just the basics and any watery situation is built up round a complete ecosystem of insects and other pond life. With luck, and if the conditions are right, dragonflies may make an appearance, their brilliant bodies and flashing wings adding more colour and movement. For many people goldfish, or more correctly golden orfe, and lilies create the mood perfectly: and the classical pool at the top of page 63 does just that. Old stone coping, a sundial and a backdrop of planting make a fitting climax to this section. Even if there is not the setting for it, somewhere, somehow, there is room for water in one of its forms, and thank goodness for that!

Streams

A pond or pool is still, whereas streams are in constant motion. In order to make this possible in a garden, the ground over which they flow must have a reasonable slope. Of all water features streams are probably the most difficult to create realistically, for where a pool can quite obviously be artificial and look none the worse for it, a stream should be as natural as possible. Lack of naturalness is, of course, the problem in most gardens with the ubiquitous 'currant bun' rockery (i.e. rocks stuck in at random) and obvious concrete or exposed liner watercourse leading to an ill-conceived pond. In many ways it is a legacy from the Victorian garden where serpentine lakes and streams imitated the features of the great landscape parks of a century earlier.

Streams should always look natural and this example uses a butyl liner that is cleverly disguised

Many people, when they think of a stream, assume, quite wrongly, that rock must be a feature. In a natural situation it might well be so, but more often than not a watercourse passes through damp lowlands with meadow and indigenous planting running down to the margins. In a large garden this can be delightful and it should be understated rather than hogging the limelight. Almost invariably a stream runs through the area already and all that is needed is a little help in the form of additional planting or judicious thinning of trees and scrub to bring things to life.

Very occasionally, it is possible to create a watercourse, but it must look natural. I took on this task once in a lovely old garden in Devon where lawns ran gently away, first into rougher grass and then into meadow. I removed the existing cattle fence and built in a ha-ha to reinforce the link between garden and landscape, then started on the stream. The length of run was something like 45 m (150 ft) – not much but an extremely delicate task. I cut the channel as realistically as possible, using the soil to create gentle contours or 'interlocking spurs' through which the stream could flow. When ground is shaped in this way, the gradients should be kept as shallow as possible, for both ease of maintenance and a realistic effect. At the end of the stream I created a pool of reasonable size, an essential feature, as it formed the reservoir from which water could be pumped to create an adequate flow. A tough butyl liner was used, both for the pool and the stream, taken well back from the margins so that turf and plants could be incorporated by the water's edge. A feed pipe in flexible plastic was also run below ground, back to the stream source, and the size of the pump had to be considerable to both lift and push the water over the distance. The source itself was concealed in a group of trees and shrubs planted on the boundaries of the property, looking for all the world as if the stream naturally entered from higher ground. The total cost of the work was several thousand pounds, a considerable sum of money but the mark of success was that few people commented on the finished scheme. It looked so totally at home that everyone took it for granted: it could have been there for thousands of years.

On page 72 I have drawn a planting plan of part of this stream. The whole secret of success is variation. A stream is not a canal and not only does it meander but it changes depth and width frequently. A steeper section encourages faster flow and this tends to produce a stony bottom that is kept clean. This natural occurance can be quite easily copied. Conversely, where the gradient decreases things slow down, silt is deposited and the margins become bigger. This is the ideal situation for marshy marginal planting. The liner is taken well back into the surrounding banks and a permeable barrier divides the stream and damp areas. I usually use rolls of turf that can be bedded down; these quickly knit into the newly established plants and the whole composition is both durable and natural.

One advantage of an artificial stream, even on this scale, over the real thing is the lack of flooding, which in a natural setting can wreak havoc with delicate planting.

This stream was formed around a concrete shell, but the rocks are so positioned to make it look naturally part of an upland area

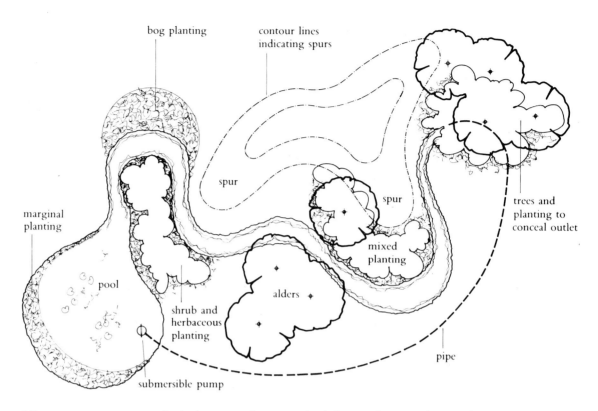

bog planting

contour lines
indicating spurs

trees and
planting to
conceal outlet

marginal
planting

spur

spur

mixed
planting

pool

alders

shrub and
herbaceous
planting

pipe

submersible pump

*Provided there is room available it is quite
possible to recreate an entirely natural looking
stream. Here the ground has been contoured to
form 'interlocking spurs', water being recirculated
by a powerful pump via a buried pipe. Planting
softens the margins and hides the tough rubber
liner*

I find this a welcome relief from the garish, crashing streams and waterfalls that totally dominate so many gardens. They are far too obvious and are, in consequence, boring. Perhaps the key question anyone should ask when planning this sort of feature is *why*? Why do I want it and why is it necessary? If you can answer these questions sensibly, it is almost certain that a practical and aesthetic composition will result.

It is hard to believe that the delightful little stream and waterfall pictured on page 67 is artificial. This is rock and water gardening at its best. For a start, the stream is laid out with the system of interlocking spurs mentioned on page 68, the watercourse zig-zagging between the outcrops. The slope is quite steep, as it would be in a typical upland area near the head of a stream. Because the flow is considerable, water runs over hard rock and then falls into a deeper pool below, the latter being cut out by erosion. Slate has a character of its own: it is laid down with strong, regular strata and should always be used so that the original pattern is repeated. In the illustration all the rocks have been set along a similar 'bedding plane', set at a slight angle. The rock in the foreground has been pushed out of place, probably by flood water at some time and this one misplaced boulder adds to the realism of the group. The stream bed is made up of shale and small stones, and the pockets and crevices are filled with soil in just the right places – those escaping the main flow when the stream is in spate. Planting completes the picture, trollius, hosta and primulas reinforcing what is a delightful pastiche. In this garden the central rock, set by the waterfall, could act as a stepping stone. No need for a bridge here: it would be quite out of keeping and quite unnecessary.

The stream on the opposite page is quite different, being placed within a contemporary garden setting. The rock here is a soft red sandstone and the stream runs from an upper pool in front of the rocks on the skyline, drops down underneath a terrace and barbecue area, built from timber decking, and issues once again under the wide timber steps that work their way up the slope. From there the stream flows through the pebbles and larger stones to fan out into the large pool in the foreground. Stepping stones carefully set in the grass provide access. The whole system again being powered by a large submersible pump, located in the pool.

This is a spring garden on acid soil and although there is a high proportion of rhododendrons and azaleas, these by no means dominate. The yellow azaleas are set in a well-placed drift along the bank, while the glaucous leaves of *Hebe pinguifolia* 'Pagei' act as both a unifying element and ground cover. The Japanese maple by the steps is a particularly fine specimen while the bowl of white tobacco plants (forced at this time of the year) makes a particularly telling statement, set at the edge of the decking. This acts as a focal point and has the eminently practical job of guarding the drop, far better than some hideous railing, or even a timber screen to match the deck and steps.

A small stream is easily crossed by a step or a jump, but anything wider than 90 cm (3 ft) is going to need a bridge, something totally sympathetic.

Where there is water, bridges become a distinct possibility. The styles are legion, but be sensitive, respecting local materials and techniques. Handrails often hint at municipal bureaucracy – in a domestic garden they are rarely necessary

Striking view of the stream in the rock garden at Wisley, the Royal Horticultural Society's centre in Surrey

I have seen some fine bridges that simply look ridiculous in a particular setting. There is still a trend towards rustic work that has been with us in Britain for some 150 years, and is to be avoided if possible, for not only does it rot quickly but it is simply unsuitable in the vast majority of cases.

The type of bridge is determined by a number of factors, including its span, the amount of use it is likely to get, the character of the surroundings and, not least, the budget available – bridges can be expensive. On page 69

is shown a number of quite different examples.

If the flow is particularly slow it might be possible to cross the water by a series of logs driven into the ground, like piles. Obviously the trunks need to be butted as closely as possible, and an intricate pattern can be built up. Such an approach is informal and it would look too rigid if the walkway has sharply parallel sides. A random pattern that lets the timber drift off on either side is preferable. A link of this kind is really a hybrid, halfway between a path and a bridge, and it would look particularly good surrounded by aquatic acid waterside species. The ideal situation, apart from one with slow water flow, would be where minimal disruption to a view is needed. A hand rail is quite unnecessary. It is, in fact, the obsession with safety that ruins many a bridge, both public and domestic. It may be justified where pedestrian traffic is heavy but in a garden, or low-use area, a rail often gets in the way of both the line of structure and the view. If a rail is needed, it should be constructed from sympathetic materials and emphasize rather than detract from the overall composition. This can be achieved by continuing the railing on either side, letting it run into the planting so that the ends are concealed. This treatment follows another of those underlying rules of landscape and garden design: never slap a feature down anywhere and always make sure it is integrated into the overall garden pattern.

The point at which a bridge crosses water is also important: relate it to

Key to planting plan

1	1	*Rheum palmatum* 'Tanguticum'
2	7	*Hosta sieboldiana*
3	8	*Primula florindae*
4	8	*Astilbe × arendsii* 'Fanal'
5	9	*Primula denticulata*
6	4	*Rogersia aesculifolia*
7	7	*Filipendula purpurea*
8	2	*Aruncus sylvester*
9	7	*Iris siberica* 'Thelma Perry'
10	1	*Kirengeshoma palmata*
11	5	*Lysichitum americanum*
12	5	*Filipendula ulmaria* 'Variegata'

Streams require specialised planting that will thrive in moist conditions. Such permanent damp allows the cultivation of a vast range of spectacular species, many of which have the most striking flower and foliage

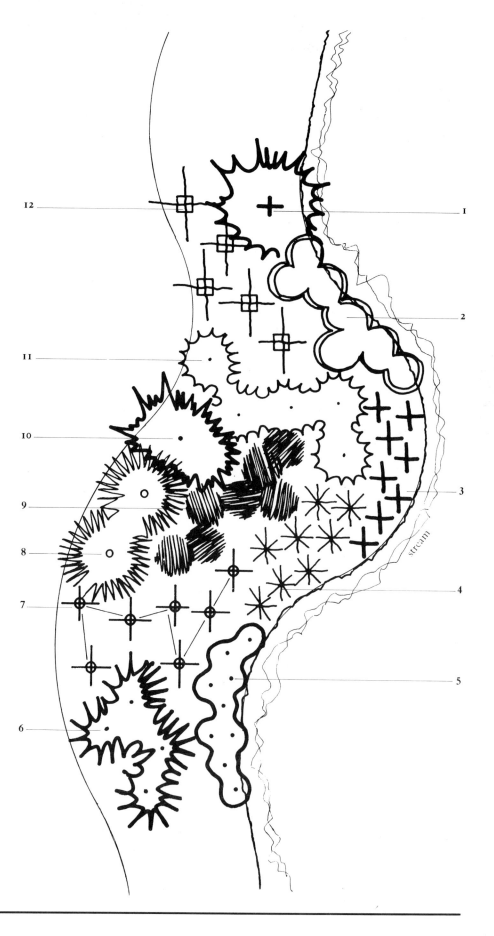

the land form on either side and, finally, think of colour. The latter should usually be undemonstrative, a simple stain being often most effective. Sometimes – with care – colour can be made a real point of emphasis. In the courtyard of a very modern house I once painted a simple low bridge dark blue, linking it into a background of grey paving, grey and purple planting and the smoked glass of the building itself. The result was breathtaking.

The last bridge illustrated here is essentially Japanese and has that simple line and unfussy construction that make it a piece of pure sculpture. It always seeems remarkable that a few crisp boards and solid square uprights can be turned into the most handsome structure. Part of this bridge's success lies in the fact that it is both horizontal and low, appearing to be as one with the water, rather than an object slung over it. The traditional Japanese bridge, of which this is a copy, has religious significance and is supposed to prevent the devil from running across it: the inept spectre is unable to negotiate the pattern of staggered boards and falls helpless into the water, and is, presumably, as feeble at swimming as he is at crossing bridges!

The photograph on page 71 reminds me of another legend: Kipling's story about how the elephant got his trunk. This stream simply must be the headwaters of the great grey-green greasy Limpopo River all set about with – well, if not fever trees, at least the fronds of Japanese maple and the bold leaves of rhododendron. I think this is the most atmospheric of the streams shown here. The stepping stones, all smooth and wet, look like the backs of turtles and the water issuing from the bank must make just the right noise as it falls into the pool below. This is one of those secret places in the garden, somewhere to pause and meditate; children would love it. Like many parts of the garden that work well, I suspect a great deal of time, thought and effort has gone into making this a success. It is like that stream in Devon, people would take it for granted.

Finally the illustration on page 70 is part of that great English garden at Wisley, in Surrey, home of the Royal Horticultural Society. I am not enthusiastic about a lot of Wisley but there are parts of it that are sheer poetry, and this is one of them. It is in many ways the sort of rock and stream garden that is the starting-point for so many failures in domestic situations. Its strength lies in the size and boldness of the rock outcrops. Each piece must weigh many thousand kilograms (several tons) and they are very well set in a pattern that allows ample scope for the stream to cascade from level to level. Here, unlike most rockeries, the stone is difficult to see and this is why the composition succeeds. It is, after all, the planting that is important: the rockery simply provides a frame and growing medium.

One of the problems here is access: maintenance is far from easy and invasion by weeds is always a nuisance in this sort of area. To my mind a rockery is probably the most labour-intensive part of a garden.

The planting, however, is worth it, a background of ferns interlaced with hostas, primulas and astilbe. Indeed a delightful picture.

Bog Gardens

Above: *The bog garden at Great Saling Hall in Essex.* Opposite: *Another of view of Beth Chatto's magnificent garden*

'Bog' is hardly the most inspirational name for a part of the garden that can, perhaps, be more attractive than any other. It is not a natural habitat that is found in the average domestic plot, although many of the specialist water garden nurseries and garden centres would have us believe that it is.

Plants that thrive close to water fall into a number of classifications, according to their requirements, although to all intents and purposes they appear as a continuous band of vegetation. First there are those at the highest level: they need ample moisture for their spring and summer growing season, but cannot tolerate completely waterlogged soil or ground that is only occasionally wet – say, during winter. These plants need both air and water, the ideal situation being the bank of a pond, stream or river where roots are above the water table but able to draw moisture from below if necessary. Most such plants are hardy perennials and although a typical waterside is rich in such species, they are separate from the true marsh plants lower down.

Marsh or bog plants have adapted themselves to tolerate permanently or predominantly saturated soil, a fact that makes them far more suitable for garden use. Finally there are the true marginals that need always to be covered by 2.5–5 cm (1–2 in) of water; in a natural environment this would include the rushes and maces.

In the countryside, a river or stream will often contain plants in all these classifications, but the steeper the banks, the less room there is available. This, of course, is the problem faced by conservationists who are continually fighting battles with river authorities to provide sensitive deepening and widening schemes. If a river is dredged with steep banks, then there is little room for natural species to develop. The traditional water meadow with shallow margins may create flood control problems but it was home for great sweeps of iris and marsh marigolds that were once far more widespread than the boring, straight canals so often seen today.

In a garden the destiny of plants can be controlled and suitable conditions provided to a pattern that fits in with the overall design criteria.

The merits of using a plastic or butyl liner rather than concrete have already been discussed in the chapter on ponds; the ideal bog garden will simply require a continuation of the sheet to cover the additional area required. Incidentally, butyl liners are made from wide strips of material welded together, and it is therefore relatively easy to obtain a sheet of the required size. The point to bear in mind is the overall shape of the pool and surrounding marginal area. A simple shape that requires little trimming will be more economical than a pattern that has irregular or awkwardly shaped edges. In fact, natural ponds usually have uncluttered lines, which enhance rather than detract from their surroundings. It is only in an artificial situation that complication sets in. Perhaps the worst enemy of a successful garden is the preoccupation with design for design's sake – in vulgar parlance, 'tarting up'! Pools and water gardens are particularly susceptible to this treatment, and it is to be avoided if possible.

Virtually any garden can be a host to bog plants and the ideal situation would, indeed, be a natural spring or stream. An area that is simply wet in winter, although tempting, is quite wrong, as it is likely to dry out at the height of summer, precisely when plants most need moisture. A continuation of a pool or pond is ideal however, as the water level can remain constant or, if it drops because of evaporation, can be easily raised.

The ideal pool has a marginal shelf approximately 22.5 cm (9 in) below water level to accommodate the appropriate plants. If this shelf is extended, preferably generously, to a width of between 0.9 and 1.8 m (3 and 6 ft) it becomes the basis of a perfect marsh. It can be filled with topsoil varying in depth from just below water level to some 15–30 cm (6–12 in) above it. This will allow for a changing habitat to suit the widest possible range of species. A wide shelf makes access necessary and broad stepping stones should be provided so that all parts can be maintained easily. Where the shelf drops down to the deeper parts of the pond there will obviously be a need to retain the soil, and an edge of stone, brick, or occasionally peat

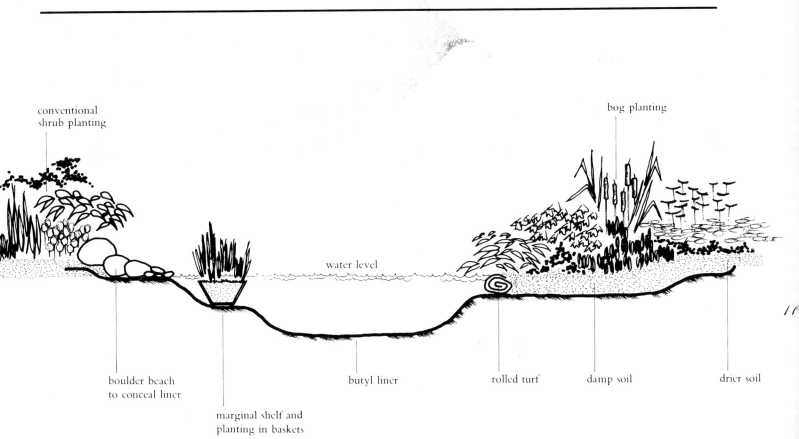

conventional
shrub planting

bog planting

water level

boulder beach
to conceal liner

butyl liner

rolled turf

damp soil

drier soil

marginal shelf and
planting in baskets

blocks, can form a definite boundary. This should be slightly below the surface so that water can seep over the top of it. It is also advisable, if brick is being used to leave open joints every so often.

The use of a butyl liner to form the pool and associated marsh garden is advisable, but an old concrete pond that has developed hairline cracks or leaks can form a ready-made bog. As it is unable to hold water, it should be filled with good quality topsoil mixed with peat, and watered to make it throughly wet. It will, of course, need topping up from time to time but it is a sensible alternative to the arduous job of digging out the whole feature.

A third possiblity is to create a self-contained bog garden without an adjoining pool. Here the aim is to slow the flow of water down, rather than stopping it altogether. Excavate an adequate area, approximately 30 cm (12 in) deep. Over the bottom, place a perforated polthyene sheet or spread a layer of wet clay, worked to the consistency of putty. The sides of the garden should not be lined, so that moisture can seep away instead of becoming stagnant. A 15-cm (6-in) layer of peaty loam should be placed over the bottom and a length of pierced hose, with one end blocked off is laid over the loam, with the other end open and projecting above the surrounding ground level. The bed should be topped up with more loam and in dry weather the hose should be connected to a water supply, so as to keep the garden permanently moist.

The technical details of how to create the right environment may sound mundane, but one rule of landscape design is that it is the unseen things that really count and that makes gardens thrive: do the groundwork and the rest follows naturally. These are the nuts and bolts of gardening. The

To create a bog, water has to be filtered from a pool or stream into a permanently damp area. This can be done with a line of loosely-laid bricks or stone. Perhaps the most natural technique is to use rolls of turf, with the grass inside. This will knit into a rapidly developing root system to form a matt of root and foliage

Three gardens for moisture-loving plants:
Top: *The Rookery at Streatham.* Above:
Burford House. Opposite: *York Gate*

enjoyment comes with the planting and in the chosen waterside gardens here there is a wide range of mood and environment. The picture on the left of this page was taken in the grounds of Burford House, in the county of Hereford and Worcester. This is the type of waterside habitat first mentioned, wet but not waterlogged, with plenty of additional oxygen available for the plants, among them primulas and iris. Nothing difficult or choosy here, simply plants that do well. The colour too is just right, a strong pink, rather than the more usual bland colour, which looks perfect against the pale purple. Ferns, indispensible lovers of wet and not-so-wet land, form a sensible background a little higher on the slope, where a constant water supply is not so critical.

The illustration at the top of this same page is on an altogether larger scale and shows not just a damp situation in the foreground, but a well-planted garden climbing the surrounding slopes. Often one of the most attractive features of a bog garden is that it is set in a dell, so that one comes upon it as something of a surprise. This is precisely what happens here: the informal stone steps drop down past the architectural mahonia, planted in a relatively dry position. On the other side of the path mature rhododendrons will make a superb spring display, underlining the point that planting should provide colour and interest throughout the seasons. Day lilies are indispensible, thriving almost anywhere, including boggy conditions. The yellow provides a visual link with the red hot pokers, an unusual but effective choice that provides emphasis and is echoed by the vertical line of the grasses. Primulas, iris and astilbe complete the picture: a

perfectly relaxed and thoroughly English setting, whose charm is increased by the movement and the sound of water on a hot summer day.

Background planting that enhances a waterside setting is very important indeed. There is nothing worse than a feature in isolation, whether it is a statue, rockery or pool. Any such focal point – for this is what they are – should be tied into the overall garden plan. By the waterside, shrubs such as cornus, willow and bamboo will create that tie, while at higher levels, alder, poplar and that marvellous deciduous conifer, swamp cypress, will make the perfect natural link with a larger landscape setting.

Of all the waterside photographs shown here, to my mind the winner is the charming composition at Great Saling Hall in Essex, on page 74. The juxtaposition of flower and foliage is irresistible. There is a perfect range of habitats, from the high bank on one side to the saturated ground by the water. The foreground group of *Viburnum davidii*, with its leathery evergreen leaves, is backed by a variegated hosta and flanked by the sculptural ligularia. Bog primulas, more hostas and ferns fill the middle distance, while that old stalwart, gunnera, rears its huge leaves out of the shade in the distance. The tree in the middle is in fact swamp cypress with its singing green spring foliage, only outdone by its autumnal display. The lawn slides down the slope, and the steps are angled so that they focus naturally on the little statue in the middle of the pool. The dark background of trees adds a note of mystery, another essential design element when constructing bog gardens.

This setting is finely controlled; the illustration (of Beth Chatto's garden) on the opposite page is altogether softer. Planned certainly, but with the touch of the plantswomen rather than the architect. It is an interesting divergence in style and undoubtedly successful. In many ways it is a much more natural setting: no lawns crisply mown, down by the water's edge here, but an almost random cascade of foliage that is nevertheless carefully planned. It is, apart from certain of the introductions, precisely the sort of river margin you would hope to find in the countryside. There are plenty of old favourites here but the association of the marigolds and the water forget-me-nots is charming.

Because damp, watery margins are such favourable growing conditions for certain species, any material should be chosen carefully. In particular, bulrush and the flowering rush (butomus), typha (reedmace) and cyperus and glyceria are so rampant that they could quickly overwhelm other less vigorous but more attractive species. If they are chosen – and they can be attractive in certain areas – they should be housed in containers that will limit their spread.

There are a number of other superb plants that are, for lack of space, not shown in any of the illustrations here. A must, if there is room, is *Lysichitum americanum*, which bears massive yellow flowers, like those of the cuckoo pint; a less common white variety, *L. camtschatcense*, is also very worthwhile. All the mimulus (musk) are a natural choice, with a range of flower colour from yellow through crimson to the vivid red and

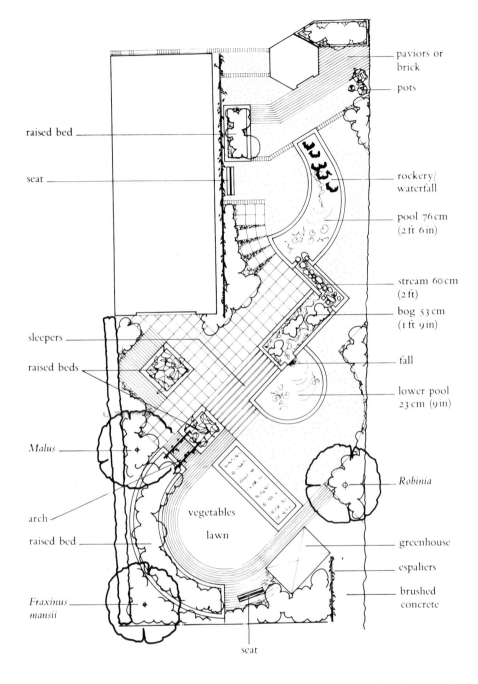

pots

raised bed

seat

rockery/ waterfall

pool 76cm (2 ft 6 in)

stream 60 cm (2 ft)

bog 53 cm (1 ft 9 in)

sleepers

raised beds

fall

lower pool 23 cm (9 in)

Malus

Robinia

arch

raised bed

greenhouse

espaliers

Fraxinus mansii

brushed concrete

vegetables

lawn

seat

This is a garden for handicapped people. It includes an unusual water feature which is raised along its entire length. A stream issues from rocks at the highest point, descending through loose stones and cobbles and a bog garden before terminating in a large pool

yellow blotched leaf of the invasive *Mimulus guttatus*. Lastly, there is the charming eriphorum, commonly called bog cotton or cotton grass. It thrives in waterlogged soil and has white tufts on grassy stems, which can grow to just over 30 cm (1 ft) long.

The final photograph on page 79 is a fitting end to this section: a garden on a sloping site through which a stream gently filters. No crashing waterfalls but a wealth of flower and foliage that has knitted together to reduce maintenance to a minimum, including trollius with its yellow buttercup flowers, soft pink primulas, ferns, bamboo and the ever dependable glaucous hosta, at home in so many situations, but particularly happy by the edge of a stream, bog or pool.

GARDENS FOR A PLANTSMAN

In the introduction of this book I said that it was impossible to define the term 'plantsman'. Is it someone who has a wealth of botanical knowledge, or the knack of using propogation and growing techniques? Is it a feeling for mood, colour and juxtaposition, or rather for what can be achieved in a garden with ideal growing conditions? I would certainly eliminate this definition: plantsmen have created magic out of chaos. My suggestion is that it is a combination of all the other definitions. A plantsman or woman is a rare person, a 'natural' possessing the attributes of designer, horticulturalist and nurseryman, and using them to create gardens of great individuality. Often such people are perfectionists and I guess that this discourages them from entering into the commercial world of growing plants for a living. Just occasionally somebody is both plantsman and commercial grower, to the great benefit of all gardeners. My own hero is Alan Bloom, that master craftsman of hardy perennials, whose Dell garden at Bressingham in Norfolk has influenced thousands of visitors. Alan Bloom's passion for plants has brought pleasure to many and led to the development of many new varieties. In addition, he has strengthened the position of herbaceous plants to a point where they are no longer threatened by the ubiquitous shrub and the stigma of high maintenance, which nearly put paid to them a few years ago.

Like horticulture itself, plantsmen fall into any number of catagories. Some may specialize in a single area or species – alpines or heathers, for instance. Others work with the whole spectrum of plants, weaving them into a living tapestry: Gertrude Jekyll was just such a person. Where room is available the scale of that tapestry can extend to woodland or even landscape. The creation of an arboretum is just as important as putting plants into an old stone sink: one is a giant, the other a gem. In other words it is simply a question of scale – a plantsman can make things work at either end, in an intimate or expansive situation.

Another interesting aspect is the time scale involved: a small border can be seen at a single glance, a woodland may take an hour to walk through. Both contain a mass of detail to be absorbed over a far longer period that changes with the seasons.

Another major difference between someone hooked on plants – for that is precisely what plantsmen are – and the average garden owner, is the amount of maintenance each is prepared to undertake. While the most of us hope to do the minimum and plan towards that end, the real enthusiast is totally dedicated. All passions are consuming and many of them gain their reward in a wealth of knowledge. The plantsman's knowledge is translated into drawing plants together in perfect harmony. This section deals with just a few of the countless examples of this.

Pots and climbers can bring a paved area to life, not only by providing instant colour and interest but by helping to link the transition between house and garden. In the picture opposite 'plantsmans pots' have that subtle balance of form and foliage that bring the composition to life

The Flower Garden

There can be hardly anyone who at some time or other has not taken plants or flowers from a garden to use as decoration inside the house. In economic terms home-produced plant material is far cheaper than what is sold in florists and it makes sense to encourage species that can be used for decoration. It so happens that many plants suitable for flower arranging are particularly handsome in their own right and are likely to impose an overall theme on a garden if grown in any quantity. It therefore follows that people interested in floral art are going to be preoccupied with the line, colour and shape of shrubs and hardy perennials: they will, in effect, be plantsmen. Such gardeners gain a close understanding of not just one phase of a plant's development – say, its flower – but of every aspect of its growth, from delicate spring foliage, right through to brilliant autumn colour, seed heads and berries. Each of these stages can be used for arrangements, in conjunction with other species. The mixture in a vase often reflects a similar combination in the garden, an overall pattern built up in a sensitive rather than a brash or unplanned way.

It is often argued that plantsmen's gardens are too full of plant material,

Key to planting plan

1   3 *Hebe* 'Midsummer Beauty'
2   1 *Hibiscus syriacus* 'Woodbridge'
3   2 *Yucca filamentosa*
4   2 *Choisya ternata*
5   1 *Clerodendron trichotomum*
6   3 *Potentilla fruticosa* 'Katherine Dykes'
7   4 *Cytisus* × *purpureus*
8   13 *Hebe pinguifolia* 'Pagei'
9   5 *Festuca scoparius*
10   5 *Euphorbia wulfenii*

A section of border for a sunny position which utilises plants chosen for their shape and texture as much as their flower

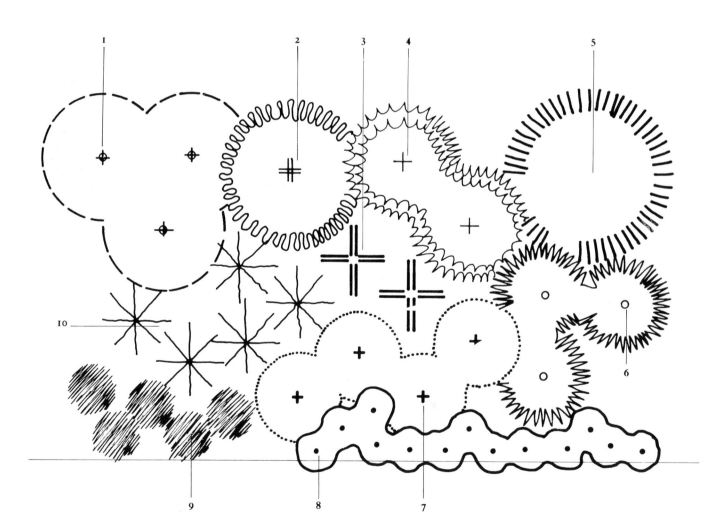

but I disagree. Most experts are fully aware of the underlying principles of garden design and use a combination of hard and soft landscape to build a whole composition. The use of paths and paved areas is essential, not just for access but also for stability. The point is that particular plants associate best with a particular theme and reinforce the underlying pattern of that theme. *Rosa rubrifolia*, a marvellous plant for arrangements, with its stem, colour, form and foliage, looks perfect in an informal setting, against a backdrop of grass and surrounding plants. The sword-like leaves of phormium, the architectural line of acanthus or the forceful character of *Euphorbia wulfenii*, on the other hand, are ideal foils for paving of any kind.

Another way in which a well-planted garden achieves its goal is through continuity. Often a drift of plant material is needed to provide a continuing supply: there is nothing worse than denuding a single specimen to leave a gaping hole in a border. A sweep of foliage or colour leads the eye through a space, or round a corner, where a vast range of individual items do not. Incidentally, the practice of growing flowers 'for

Key to planting plan

1   4 *Helleborus corsicus*
2   1 *Rheum palmatum*
3   2 *Pulmonaria saccharata*
4   2 *Dicentra eximia*
5   3 *Euphorbia epithymoides (polychroma)*
6   14 *Ajuga reptans* 'Atropurpurea'
7   3 *Dicentra eximia*

A collection of hardy perennials arranged in a plan of the garden on page 86. All these plants are suitable for shade, often a problem for so many gardeners

Subtle shades of purple and green combine in what is essentially a plantsman's collection. Although this is quite superb there would be little in the way of winter interest

cutting' in serried ranks is counter-productive in my view. Why hide them away when they can be worked into the overall composition? The technique is one left over from the days of great estates, where a staff of gardeners dug, staked and tied with little knowledge of the potential of the plants they were handling.

Good planting design is often low key. This does not in any way preclude originality or subtlety: it simply provides harmony. The opening illustration in this section, on page 82, is devastatingly simple but full of charm. The old York stone path allows access without being too obvious, acting as a foil to the mellow brick of the house. Planting here is largely seasonal, and the blending of colour is quite delightful. Strong tones are provided by the dark red tobacco plants, one of the best annuals both for filling a border and for scent. The latter is an essential part of any garden and on a warm summer evening when the windows are open, nothing is more delightful than the fragrance of these old-fashioned flowers. Further down the scale in both height and colour, the pink pelargoniums act as a perfect link between the nicotiana and the white roses that twist their way up the wall. Climbers are essential in this sort of situation and the roses are supplemented by clematis and wisteria, which flower at different times and so extend seasonal interest. Agapanthus and iris leaves provide a soft green underplanting while the bold leaves of bergenia, a plantsman's plant if ever there was one, temper the lines of the path in the distance. It could be argued that there is very little here in the winter, but in my own garden I relish the tracery of stems almost as much as the lush summer growth. There is something crisp and well-ordered about an empty border in the winter, forked over and topped dressed, that gives it an air of expectancy.

On a totally different scale and creating a quite different mood is the superb grouping above. This, too, is a seasonal planting that would look at its best in late spring and early summer. All the plants are dear to my heart

Above: *A combination of sculptural plants that include euphorbia, alchemilla,* Magnolia grandiflora *and that superb climber* Actinidia kolomikta, *all help to temper the line of this delightful courtyard*

Left: *So often the view out into a garden is ignored but in this case it is heightened by the clipped yews and sprawling helianthemums. Here at Barnsley House, the land outside the garden has been drawn into the composition by the inclusion of a wrought-iron gate*

and I have them in my garden, although in different combinations. The sculptural leaves of the rheum at the back work wonders against the pale yellow bracts of euphorbia. Dicentra (bleeding heart) works its way through the front of the group and it is worth making the point that the whole of this area is in shade, a situation so many people find problematical. In fact, among plants there are as many shade lovers as there are sun worshippers: it is simply a matter of discovering which is which. Such planting as this reduces maintenance to a minimum, so much shadow is being cast by the overhanging leaves.

It is the ability to create groupings such as this that makes plantsmen different, but there are many simple combinations that can be learnt very quickly and that work every time. One of them is the contrast between rounded and upright shapes. The great spurge, *Euphorbia wulfenii*, planted next to the fastigiate Irish yew, *Taxus baccata* 'Fastigiata', make an effect that is handsome yet easy. A slightly more complex, but still simple group consists of three rounded broom at the back or middle of a border, a phormium or yucca slightly to one side and a sweep of *Hebe pagei* or potentilla 'Red Ace' in the foreground. This will always look good and underlines the point that there are most certainly basic rules of garden design: depart from them and things quickly become a mess. The purple smoke bush, *Cotinus coggygria* 'Foliis Purpureis', planted beneath a golden-leafed *Robinia pseudoacacia* 'Frisia' creates an effect that needs no description.

The scope and skill of Beth Chatto's work has already been illustrated here. She is another of those plantswomen who runs a business selling fine useful material. Her own garden could hardly have been called hospitable when she first started to cultivate it. It stands on high Essex ground and for those who know East Anglia, there is no need to underline just how cold the winters and how parched the summers can be. The soil was not good and the changes of level were such as would have discouraged many people. Perhaps the greatest lesson that can be learnt from the now near perfect acres is that Beth Chatto has respected the underlying soil and climatic conditions, selecting material that is not only tolerant of them but positively thrives in them. Of course, any ground, particularly poor soil, needs organic feeding and that is precisely what it has got over the years.

In the section on water were two views of Beth Chatto's ponds (see pages 62 and 75). Originally there was only a spring, but a great deal of hard labour brought the pools into being and the margins blossomed. At the top of page 91 is a more general view, with damp land in the foreground. Apart from the yellow-flowered trollius there is very little in the way of flower colour here, simply the contrast of leaf shapes and textures. Most of the plants are hardy perennials, but the backdrop of trees and the strongly modelled conifers stabilize the garden during the dormant season.

Gardening books that only have illustrations of gardens viewed from outside become boring. We all spend a great deal of time indoors and are going to be looking through windows for much of the time. Most

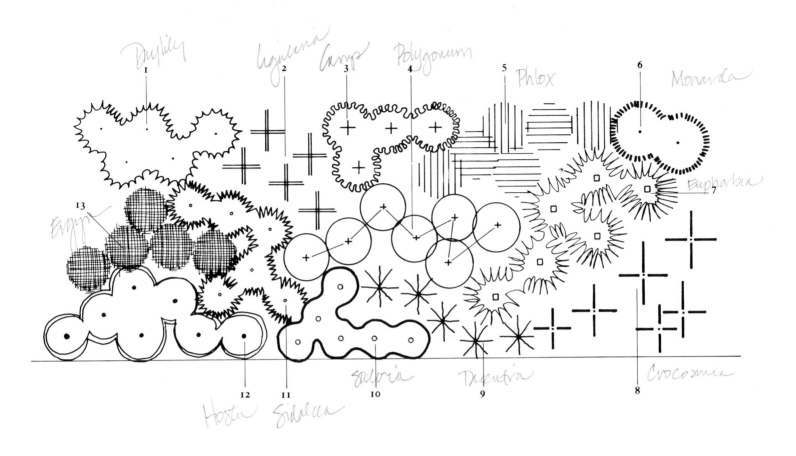

A planting of hardy perennials in full sun. This is classic herbaceous planting that although reasonably labour-intensive certainly provides a wealth of interest throughout the summer

gardens are planned without taking this basic point into account. The result is often a downright dull, if not positively ugly, view from the kitchen window – quite inexcusable. The picture at the bottom of page 87 is the reverse of dull. It is exceptionally dramatic, a piece of pure sculpture. The window, left refreshingly bare of curtains, looks like a Mondrian painting, subdivided into rectangles by the delicate glazing bars. It frames a receding line of fastigiate yews, each of which has a character of its own. The path is a path only in name: it would be impossible to tramp that route regularly through a sea of sprawling helianthemums. They are even more telling set against the stern evergreen trees that emphasize the distant gate.

Humour is not often associated with gardening, which is a pity. As soon as I saw this avenue of yews I thought of the 'twelve apostles' at Dartington Hall in Devon. These are a line of 12 fine old clipped yews that, although cut to look alike, have taken on individual personalities. Viewed from a distance they seem to nod and chat to one another in a never-ending conversation that is likely to continue for many hundreds of years.

Although foliage and form are important tools in the plantsman's hand, colour should not be forgotten. There are two broad rules: use mass rather than unrelated spots of colour and work with two basic colour ranges: blue or yellow. The blue contains white, blue, pink, crimson, purple, grey and those glaucous colours, of which *Hosta sieboldiana* is the classic example. The yellow sector includes orange, scarlet, cream, lime green,

Key to planting plan

1   5 *Hemerocallis* 'Bonanza'
2   5 *Ligularia stenocephala* 'The Rocket'
3   4 *Campanula alliarifolia* 'Ivory Bells'
4   7 *Polygonum amplexicaule* 'Atrosanguineum'
5   6 *Phlox* 'Prospero'
6   2 *Monarda* 'Blue Stocking'
7   6 *Euphorbia epithymoides (polychroma)*
8   6 *Crocosmia* 'Lucifer'
9   5 *Dicentra exima*
10   6 *Salvia superba* 'East Freisland'
11   6 *Sidalcea* 'William Smith'
12   7 *Hosta sieboldiana*
13   5 *Eryngium planum*

Like gardens, all planting schemes are different but the lesson to be learnt from these three illustrations is the fact that material is used in drifts rather than individual spots of unrelated colour. More often than not this approach also reduces maintenance as groups of a species knit together quickly to form a sweep of ground cover

apricot and those wonderful yellow/gold variegated foliage colours. This is the palette and the pictures can of course be painted in every season from spring to winter, which makes for enormous interest at the expense of complication. These two rules are not necessarily rigid: nature is far too diverse for that, but if they are kept overall then success, if not assured, is at least brought within grasp.

The perfect application of the principles of colour is shown at the bottom of page 91. This is essentially a blue range containing pink, purple and white. Cream is always something of a cross-over colour: it works well in either range and the plumes of *Aruncus sylvester* at the back merge with the white and pink closer to the foreground. As a contrast the poppies jump out, but in a thoroughly justifiable way. As a background the dark green hedge is ideal and it is worth remembering that an inherently 'active' border with plenty of interest needs to be set against a stable rather than a distracting view.

pink
purple
white
cream

Above: *Beth Chatto is of course well known for her sensitivity when handling plants. Hosta, Rogersia, Trollius and Astilbe all combine to form a delightful combination in an essentially damp area.*

Left: *The perfect application of the principles of colour, at Jenkyn Place*

Astilbe
Rogersy
Phlox

BND

Key to planting plan

1	2 *Ceanothus veichianus*
2	1 *Griselinia littoralis*
3	1 *Elaeagnus pungens* 'Maculata'
4	1 *Acer palmatum* 'Atropurpureum'
5	2 *Eriobotrya japonica*
6	3 *Arundinaria nitida*
7	2 *Arundinaria japonica*
8	1 *Hedera helix* 'Glacier'
9	1 *Acer negundo* 'Variegata'
10	1 *Acer palmatum* 'Dissectum Atropurpureum'
11	10 *Alchemilla mollis*
12	annuals in urn
13	1 *Phormium tenax* 'Variegata'
14	1 *Pittosporum tenuifolium*
15	2 *Griselinia littoralis* 'Variegata'
16	3 *Geum* × *borisii*
17	1 *Liriodendron tulipifera* 'Aureomarginata'
18	3 *Saponaria officinalis* 'Rosea Plena'
19	2 *Mahonia lomariifolia*
20	1 *Salix caprea* 'Kilmarnock'
21	2 bay trees in tubs
22	1 *Polygonatum multiflorum*
23	2 *Rhodendron* 'Pink Pearl'
24	2 *Fatsia japonica* 'Variegata'
25	1 *Robinia pseudoacacia* 'Frisia'
26	2 *Aruncus sylvester*
27	1 *Acer platanoides* 'Variegata'
28	2 *Cornus alba* 'Elegantissima'
29	1 *Cordyline australis*
30	4 *Viburnum plicatum* 'Mariesii'
31	1 *Fagus sylvatica* 'Purpurea Pendula'
32	6 *Hebe pinguifolia* 'Pagei'
33	2 *Elaeagnus ebbingii*
34	2 *Hosta fortunei* 'Aureomarginata'
35	1 *Rheum palmatum*
36	6 *Geranium pratense* 'Mrs Kendall Clarke'
37	8 *Euonymus fortunei* 'Emerald and Gold'
38	1 *Hedera canariensis* 'Gloire de Marengo'
39	12 marguerite daisies
40	8 Japanese azaleas (pink)
41	4 *Polygonum bistorta* 'Superbum'
42	1 *Acer palmatum* 'Dissectum'
43	3 *Hosta lancifolia*
44	1 *Hosta fortunei* 'Picta'
45	2 *Photinia robusta*
46	1 *Hosta undulata* 'Erromena'
47	2 *Hosta fortunei* 'Aureomarginata'
48	3 *Pulmonaria saccharata* 'Highdown'

This is the planting plan of the garden shown on the left of page 59. It is an architectural composition that reflects the underlying geometry of the design

Euphorbias have already been mentioned as 'architectural' plants, and the enormous bracts of spurge stand out against the walls and paving of the garden at the top of page 87. I find the foreground pink rather distracting here, for there is so much power in the foliage, that little else is needed. This is very much a designer's garden: in direct contrast to the leathery leaves of the *Magnolia grandiflora*, on the background wall, is *Actinidia kolomikta* on the other side, a remarkable climbing plant. Its leaves are splashed with a combination of pink and cream, as if someone had literally thrown paint over it.

The furniture is well chosen, too, not the uncomfortable and boring seats that often detract from rather than enhance a garden. To my mind, a sitting area should be a focal point and the obviously comfortable white chairs in the illustration are just that.

Finally, three quite different styles of planting all contained within a single garden at Heslington Manor, York. The first, at the top left of page

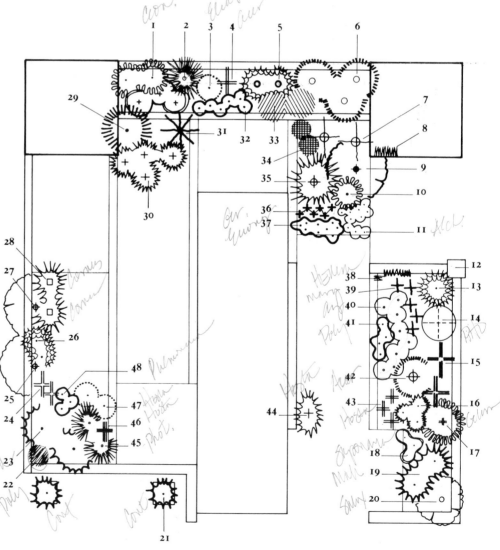

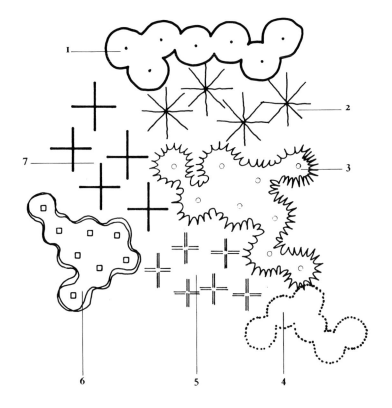

Key to planting plan

1   7 *Rheum alexandrae*
2   4 *Filipendula ulmaria*
3   9 *Brunner a macrophylla* 'Langtrees'
4   12 *Sisyrinchium striatum*
5   6 *Hosta ventricosa* 'Veriegata'
6   8 *Trollius* 'Canary Bird'
7   5 *Rogersia pinnata* 'Superba'

Many people hate damp spots in the garden, but this combination would thrive in a wet situation. There are few evergreen plants that suit wetland and this combination would be at its best in early summer

90, is the smallest, a picture in contrasting leaf shapes and forms, enlivened by the red and yellow-coloured flowers and the soft pink blooms of the variegated dead nettle. The latter is a delightful plant and not excessively invasive. The flowers look like tiny orchids, repeating themselves for months. Hellebores are another winner in a foliage composition, providing flower and leaf during the most inhospitable months of the year, while the ivy 'Goldheart' continues the theme of variegation up the wall at the back of the border.

The illustration immediately to the right underlines the point that conifers are the punctuation marks in a garden. Such an upright form should have been photographed slightly further right or left of centre to produce an assymetric composition with the stunning display of paeonies. The eggy yellow broom seems a little strong although it does work well against the dark green conifer – which goes to prove that planting design is an intensely personal business.

The final illustration in the centre of the page is altogether calmer and uses poppies as an underlying theme. In the countryside they used to be seen in great drifts of intense red, but since the age of selective weedkillers the poppy population has sadly dwindled. Hybridization has brought about colour breaks in all directions but the underlying rule is still to plant poppies in sweeping masses. The flowers fade quickly but if there are enough plants, the effect can be sustained, and is very worthwhile.

It is clear that plantsmen and plantswomen work to an individual pattern. Such patterns are often different from one another, and always personal, which is what the best gardens are all about.

Above: *Wild flowers are charming and this area could be the edge of a meadow or garden where it skirts an orchard*
Right: *Green is the predominant woodland colour and this brick-paved sitting area merges into the surrounding trees. The deck chairs provide a splash of colour that lifts the design*
Opposite: *A mossy floor precludes regular walking but brings a magic of its own, softening the contours and leading the eye to the water beyond*

Woodland Gardens

Woodlands have always fascinated me: trees are, after all, the largest living things in the world. Woods and forests in the wild are dependent on a number of factors that include soil type, climate and altitude. Oak, ash and sycamore, for example, are lowland trees, while conifers dominate higher regions. Beech and yew have a liking for chalky or alkaline soils, while alder, poplar and willow thrive by the water.

In a natural situation woodland develops through a series of stages, starting with colonization by a wide range of species. Slowly, over a period of many years, these are thinned out by competition until eventually there can be a victory of a single type that dominates over all else.

In England the richest habitats are found in oak woodland, which hosts a wide range of both plant material and animal life. Beech forest is a very different matter, the floor often being practically bare. Few conifers are indigenous to the British Isles and the mass planting by the Forestry Commission, particularly of Norway spruce, has, in the visual sense, ruined vast tracts of land from Scotland to the South Coast. The unsympathetic way in which plantations are laid out is also a problem: they often cut across contours and hillsides, whereas a more sensitive approach would have followed the line of the valley or spur. In some cases this technique is now being adopted, and it maintains far greater harmony with the surrounding landscape.

Within a rich woodland, such as oak, the planting runs in definite strata with low ground cover, a middle layer of shrubs and the highest position

Timber is a natural choice for woodland steps and here both discs and logs have been used to climb a gentle slope in a thoroughly practical way

occupied by the trees themselves. This is exactly the same pattern that is used in domestic garden planning, on a smaller scale and more open situation.

Woodland has been an integral part of landscape gardening for centuries and derives from the hunting forests of the Middle Ages. The landscape school of the 18th century made idealized compositions by strategic planting and thinning but it was not until the Victorian age that wood and garden came together. This was largely due to the introduction of new plant varieties from all over the world, rhododendron playing the most important role. In fact, so much of the latter was planted that in many parts of Britain it is becoming a climax species in its own right, to the detriment of much indigenous vegetation.

A wild garden is something rather different and although most plots are simply too small to accommodate woodland, an area of, say, rough grass, naturalized with bulbs and wild flowers, is quite feasible. In fact, it can often be a positive advantage: fine lawn nearer the house running into a wild section beneath fruit trees, makes a garden look larger. In addition, rough grass need only be cut three or four times a year, reducing maintenance to a minimum. The timing, however, is critical. The first cut should be after the spring bulbs have died down but before the midsummer wildflowers, the second cut once the latter have set seed and a final mow to put the area to bed for winter. All these cuts can use a rotary mower with the blades set comfortably high. Access can be by mown paths and there is nothing more restful than meandering through an orchard in high summer. This is precisely the mood of the delightful illustration at the top of page 94, with its cow parsley, buttercups and dandelions. Apart from being a childrens paradise, a garden treated in this way is free of that over-zealous, manicured look that is the ruination of many. Why create work where none is needed?

The picture at the bottom of the same page goes a stage further. This is not the soft grass of an orchard or true woodland, but it is pretty. It is a charmingly informal sitting area floored in old stone and revolving round the centrally placed tree. Planting is essentially green and the overhead canopy is light enough to let the sun filter through, to cast a tracery of shadow. Shadow is not used nearly enough as a design element in Britain. The light is not as intense as, say, that of Mediterranean countries but it is quite strong enough to create an added dimension that can transform a paved or walled area. As a designer I particularly like the deck chairs in this illustration, the splash of red is just what is needed to inject a little extra life into the composition. I also like the simple seat that works in direct contrast, providing a stable link with the solidity of the woodland beyond.

True woodland in its entirety is shown on page 95. This is an atmospheric scene, whose effect is heightened by the soft growth of mossy grass covering the ground. It is a psychological as well as a physical success because it suggests virgin forest, largely untouched or untrodden: any

In an area where stone outcrops naturally, the use of stone can be a cheap and effective material for steps. This is an informal flight, the planting softening the outline. Never use this treatment in a suburban setting – it simply looks pretentious

Colour can be desperately difficult to handle in the spring, but the delicate cherry blossom is the perfect foil for the simply stunning azalea growing below

footfall would quickly destroy the fragile surface. In many ways this is an idyllic setting, with water, rock and trees forming a pattern that is almost too good to be true.

Access is, of course, an important matter and while a mown path is quite satisfactory through rough grass, something more permanent is often needed under trees. A formally paved route looks quite wrong and so, too, does one that runs in a straight line. What is needed is a meandering path that weaves between trees and around shrub planting to create both movement and surprise. The surface can simply be beaten soil if the area is dry enough, although one of the most successful paths I have seen used cobbles, packed tightly together. These were ideal as their size allowed them to form a route of different widths, spreading out in places to form a stitting area. Such a surface would give dry shod access and be able to be swept clear of leaves in the autumn. Another surface would be slices of hard wood such as oak or elm, the latter being particularly suitable as it is water resistant. Such stepping stones can cross planting, linking sections of path together. Often in a woodland setting there are quite steep changes in level and the theme should continue to be in sympathy with this. Log steps, bedded into the slope firmly held in place by wedges, look ideal. They need not necessarily be in a straight flight: the pattern can be staggered and planting allowed to soften the edges.

Above: *Cherries and azalea combine again in a subtle colour range that is echoed by the fallen petals. The young beech foliage helps to tone the more vibrant colour down while the twisted stems form a sculpture of their own*
Left: *Foxgloves are essential woodland plants and ideally should be left to naturalise and self-seed over a wide area*

Available timber presupposes that trees are being lopped and felled – good husbandry is absolutely essential. Tree surgery is vital to keep woodland in peak condition and work poorly carried out encourages the spread of disease. Planting too is important as a wood is a living entity in which death is a natural component. New trees, planted with care and chosen for their visual and ecological balance with the surroundings, will ensure a healthy plantation for the future.

However, the question of woodland management is an awkward one. The current trend is all for thinning, protecting and replanting to keep trees and the ground beneath them in a particular stage of development. While this can maximise the variety of flora and fauna, it is of course artificial. To my mind, if space allows, it is often more practical to allow natural development. A certain species will always climax but this takes a long time and there is a great deal of evolution along the way.

Colour does not often occur naturally in British woodlands and when it does, it is usually the blue haze of bluebells that can cover acres during the spring. It is this broad type of planting that can tie a forest floor together. Another plant that thrives on the margins of woodland and in clearings is the foxglove and a great sweep of them is shown at the bottom of page 99. This is an easy plant to grow: it self seeds anywhere, and it should be encouraged whenever possible.

Good tree surgery can do much to not only prolong the life of a specimen but improve its appearance. Always securely rope any limbs to be removed and cut off as much of the limb as possible before making the final cut

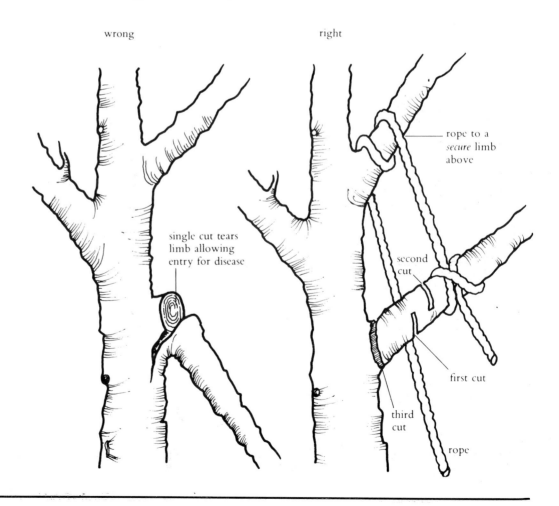

wrong

right

single cut tears limb allowing entry for disease

rope to a *secure* limb above

second cut

first cut

third cut

rope

It is the introductions that have really brought colour to British woodland gardens, rhododendron and azalea in particular. Savill Gardens in Windsor Great Park is unparalled for the number of its varieties and for depth of colour. Rhododendrons and azaleas flower early in the year, so this is particularly a spring garden.

The picture on page 98 is of Savill Gardens and shows a delicate balance between the pale green beech leaves and the more strident pink of the rhododenrons. Such colour is acceptable in small amounts, but can become overpowering in large quantities. I particularly like the carpet of fallen petals that transform the floor, if only for a short time. The illustration at the top of the opposite page is also of Savill and shows that other great spring plant, prunus. Its whiteness is a perfect foil to the stronger red below and it is sensible to let woodland plants naturalize in the way shown here, formal beds in such a situation are nonsensical and unnecessary. The practice of allowing large shrubs and trees to grow through rougher grass is a wise one. They are strong enough to do so and there is less maintenance involved. The suburban obsession for cutting out a bed around a tree in the middle of a lawn is deplorable: it destroys the underlying continuity of the grass.

To sum up: if a situation is wild – and woodland most certainly is – do not try and tame it. The result would be far from satisfactory.

Sound tree staking is essential to ensure rapid establishment. Depending on the situation select a method accordingly, the larger the tree the more support is needed

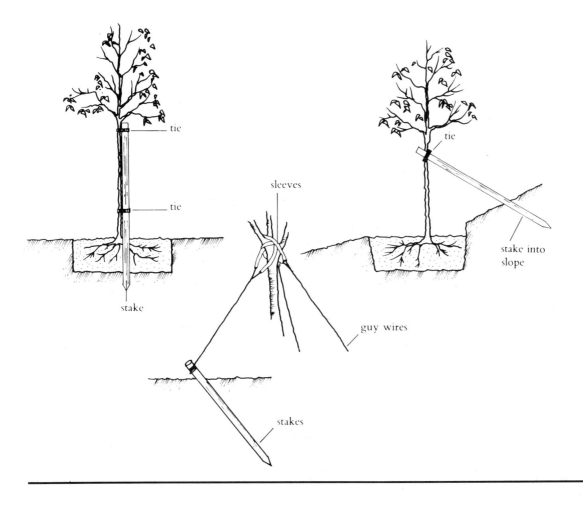

Rock and Alpine Gardens

Rocks, scree and alpine are specialist aspects of what most people would call a rockery. They are remarkably popular, which is surprising, as they are not easy to construct or maintain. The 'currant bun' rock garden degrades both the stone and the plant material in it, whereas a successful outcrop or well-planted sink can be a fascinating part of the overall garden plan and very much a focal point in its own right.

When this feature is built from scratch, there are a number of important factors to take into consideration, the first and most basic being position. Virtually all alpine plants like free draining soil and an open situation. A south or south-west aspect is ideal and if there is a natural slope so much the better. A certain amount of broken shade, from trees positioned some way away, can be beneficial, but direct drip and shade from a canopy immediately overhead is not suitable. Many gardens will, of course, face or slope the wrong way, but a north-facing bank can often be 'turned' so

Rock gardens can be difficult to handle. The example (right) at Dinmore Manor is a good English compromise: not a great deal of alpine plants but a remarkably effective composition. The rock wall (above) at Tresco Abbey in the Scilly Isles has tender plants growing in a sheltered climate not found elsewhere in Britain

Large rocks are always more effective than bits and pieces. This is a superb example of a seemingly natural watercourse and associated outcrops that leave pockets for a collection of delicate planting

that pockets of soil benefit from direct sunlight. This is simply done by setting large stones at an angle on the slope and creating virtually level planting platforms between them. The technique is shown in the diagram on page 108. Many famous gardens, including Wisley in Surrey, have made use of it to good advantage. On a perfectly level site a slope may, of course, be created by making the appropriate changes in contour: a simple mound is all too obvious; a retaining wall from which the ground gently slopes on the southern side makes a better design. It is often possible to use the 'cut and fill' technique by which soil is removed from one area to form a hollow, and stacked in another area to increase the ground level. The depression could form the site for a pool or water garden.

Another type of rock garden, and one that is altogether different, is a dry stream bed, or an imitation thereof. In part this can take on a Japanese influence and can be particularly useful in dry shady areas where plant material is difficult to establish. I have used the technique to good effect under a projecting timber deck, with large smooth stones and boulders running back under the platform. As the area moves out into easier growing conditions planting can be established and if this is incorporated with a stream the composition can be charming.

Once a position has been selected, the next question to be considered is drainage. Heavy clay soils will undoubtedly need it. Dig trenches 45 cm (1 ft 6 in) deep and approximately 1.3 m (4 ft 6 in) apart. Half fill them with broken stones, topped with upturned turves, and bring them up to the surrounding ground level with good-quality top soil. When digging trenches or creating contours, always keep top soil and subsoil separate. Subsoil is infertile and is best disposed of. Top soil if left in a stack for too long – say, six months – starts to deteriorate. Ordinary top soil alone is not ideal for a rock garden: an excellent planting medium uses 1 part of loam and peat with 2 parts of 0.6 cm ($\frac{1}{4}$ in) stone chippings, a mixture that provides the ideal 'open' texture.

The choice of rock is also critical and the temptation to use a random selection gleaned from the beach (which is, incidentally, illegal) or various parts of the garden should be resisted. It is good design practice and common sense to try to obtain a local stone if there is one. Sandstone will look far more comfortable in a sandstone area than, say, waterworn limestone. It is folly to use Westmorland rock in a Surrey garden, apart from the fact that transport costs are reflected in the retail price from a stone merchant or garden centre.

The amount and size of rock is also important. I prefer one or two bold outcrops to a mass of smaller pieces. The aim should be a direct imitation of nature, in which rock is laid down in definite strata or bands, often tilted at an angle to the horizontal by geological action. On a large scale in the landscape this forms an escarpment. In a garden the setting of the rocks should imitate this, meaning that more of the stone will be below ground than is actually visible. Anyone who keeps to the 'iceberg principle' will not go far wrong. Many rocks are formed by deposits of sediment and so are built up in layers. This pattern must be repeated in the garden and stone should never be laid so that once horizontal lines become vertical. As rocks in the landscape weather they tend to split both along the bedding planes and vertically by the action of water and frost creating blocks. In a simulated rock face, stones should never be placed like bricks in a wall, with staggered joints: such a pattern would never occur naturally. They

Rock should be set so that it appears to outcrop naturally. It should be positioned in a 'bedding plane' that remains constant and allows only a small part of the stone to be seen, the rest being below ground

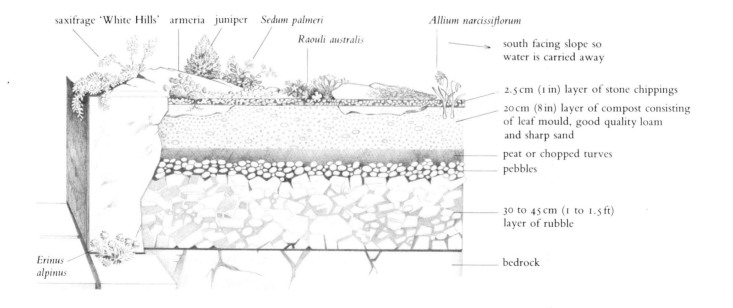

saxifrage 'White Hills' armeria juniper *Sedum palmeri*

Raouli australis

Allium narcissiflorum

south facing slope so water is carried away

2.5 cm (1 in) layer of stone chippings

20 cm (8 in) layer of compost consisting of leaf mould, good quality loam and sharp sand

peat or chopped turves

pebbles

30 to 45 cm (1 to 1.5 ft) layer of rubble

bedrock

Erinus alpinus

should be built up in irregular stacks with the occasional large stone cutting across the vertical joints, as in the diagram on page 108.

In design terms it will look very natural if the stone used in the outcrops is also used elsewhere in the garden, in level steps adjoining a rockery, for example, or in the extension of an escarpment to form a riser. The outstanding example of this is shown in the large photograph on page 102 of Dinmore Manor near Hereford. Here the stone of the rock garden matches, or is at least very similar to, that used in the background wall and arches. A point to bear in mind is that stone laid in the ground tends to pick up mosses and lichens far more quickly than stone in a wall. This is apparent in the illustration.

Dinmore Manor is by no means an alpine garden, but contains a wide range of hardy perennials and shrub material, thus reducing maintainence and providing interest through different scales of size. I like the contrasting forms of yucca, ferns, Japanese maple, bergenia and the tall, upright conifer on the right-hand side. Water provides a flat plane at the lowest level, creating interest by movement and reflection. In many ways this garden is a typical English compromise and a remarkably successful one.

My own preference is for still or gently rippling water rather than a series of crashing waterfalls. It is worth pointing out, however, that much waterworn stone is found naturally in a dry setting, since streams and rivers in upland limestone areas more often than not disappear underground. With this in mind, I looked very carefully at the photograph on page 103 and I must say that the whole feature is put together very well. These are large rocks, carefully set, and what is really important is that the watercourse itself is beautifully constructed. It cannot be said to look natural, because it would be very difficult to find such a feature in the landscape. It is, however, a real focal point and offers good growing conditions for a wide range of plants.

Raised beds or sink gardens can be ideal for growing alpine plants. Drainage is an important consideration and soil should be positioned over a base of broken stone. Weep holes must be provided or in the case of a sink the plughole kept clear

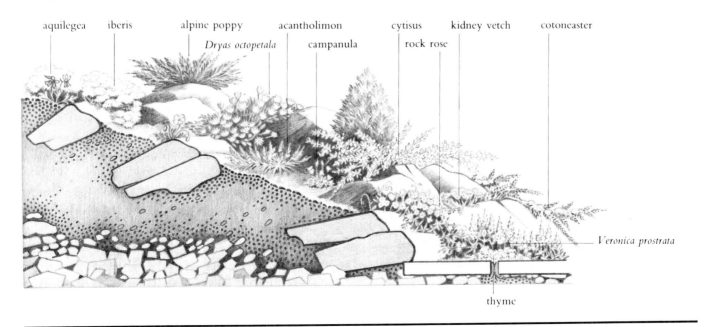

aquilegea iberis alpine poppy acantholimon cytisus kidney vetch cotoneaster
Dryas octopetala campanula rock rose

Veronica prostrata

thyme

A typical raised bed that includes both miniature conifers and alpines

An alpine and rock garden set within a larger garden. Planting and water combine to form an attractive composition that is easy to maintain

The garden in the illustration on page 103 uses mainly rock outcrops. A scree garden is rather different and reflects a more accurate picture of a true alpine setting. In any rocky or mountainous situation, stone is broken down by action of wind, frost and water into ever smaller pieces. On the way to becoming sand or soil, it passes through a stage in which chippings are formed and these are an ideal growing medium for many plants. Such species enjoy a deep, cool root run and the scree acts as a mulch during dry weather, retaining moisture. In a natural situation a scree will fan out from the base of a fissure in the rocks, and in a garden can be set between areas of rising ground. If necessary it can form an individual feature at the edge of a rockery or be quite separate, perhaps raised within a stone sink. The latter arrangement makes maintenance easy, because it cuts down on stooping. It also makes it possible to provide the ideal soil mixture.

A typical raised bed needs to be at least 45 cm (18 in) deep, with a 22.5-cm (9-in) layer of hardcore or crushed stone over the bottom. (Crushed stone comes from a non-chalky area, as many alpines will not tolerate alkaline conditions.) Over the base layer, which is there to provide good drainage, comes a layer of coarse peat or compost, 7.5–10 cm (3–4 in) deep, and lastly a topping of a scree mixture. This should be made up from 25 per cent of sharp draining sandy loam, 25 per cent leaf mould or peat and 50 per cent of 0.6-cm ($\frac{1}{4}$-in) stone chippings. It is generally thought that too free a drainage is worse than a mixture that is slightly water retentive: the recipe here should be ideal. Several large stones can be placed in the scree, adding to the overal effect of naturalness. The picture at the top of page 106 is a good example: although it contains plants other

than true alpines, including conifers, the situation is an attractive one.

It always amazes me just how tough these little alpine plants are. I have an old stone sink in my own garden, planted with species that flower at different seasons, many of them evergreen. In the winter they can be covered by many layers of snow, but after the thaw they are always there, ready to provide colour and interest for the coming season. I think it is this combination of vigour and delicate charm that won me over. In my youth I passed them by altogether.

It is, of course, possible to create a raised bed without using a stone or porcelain sink. Walling of various kinds is quite suitable and although broken precast paving in my view is unacceptable, York stone can be ideal. There is a superb old wall at Hestercombe, in Somerset, illustrated on page 107. Lavender and catmint form a delightful combination, both liking the dry, almost arid conditions. Roots will run a surprising distance in a wall and if the latter is thick it provides a cool root run in much the same way as scree. I used to share a boundary wall with a neighbour who continually exhorted me to stop planting things in it. I persisted, arguing that any possible damage would only occur long after we had both perished.

House leeks are a favourite plant of mine, surviving in almost impossible conditions that may be arid in summer and saturated in winter. There is a good example of these tough plants to the left of the picture on page 102, taken in Tresco Abbey in the Scilly Isles. To grow in such an inhospitable environment is almost miraculous, but to flower so delicately into the bargain is sheer magic. Tresco is one of the great gardens of the

An old stone wall at Hestercombe with lavender and catmint

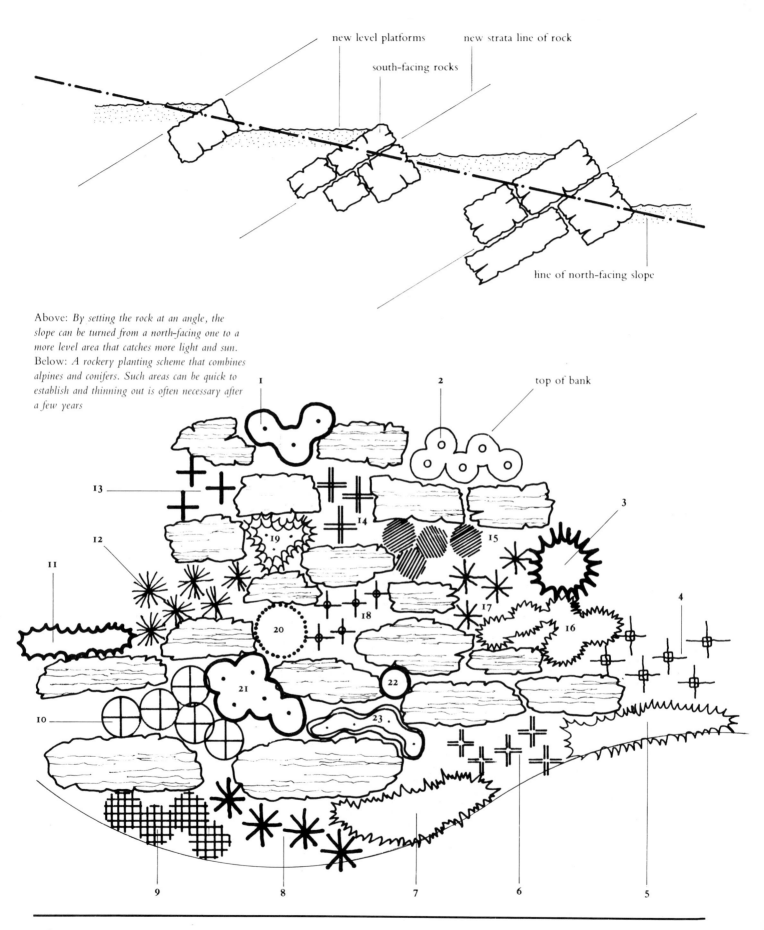

new level platforms

new strata line of rock

south-facing rocks

line of north-facing slope

Above: *By setting the rock at an angle, the slope can be turned from a north-facing one to a more level area that catches more light and sun.* Below: *A rockery planting scheme that combines alpines and conifers. Such areas can be quick to establish and thinning out is often necessary after a few years*

top of bank

British Isles. The Gulf Stream gives it an almost sub-tropical climate, supporting species that would perish on the mainland. Because of the salt-laden atmosphere the garden has an exceptionally interesting maritime collection, well worth a visit. In the illustration the splash of yellow is *Cotyledon simplifolia* that thrives on sharply draining rock walls. It is an easy plant to grow and well worth the minimal effort needed to establish it.

The photograph at the bottom of page 106, shows the attractive gardens at Froyle Mill, in Hampshire. It underlines the point that a rock garden can fit very well into the overall garden pattern. In the foreground is predominantly shrub planting that drops down the slope to the lawn, stream and pool at the bottom. The rock garden is constructed on a gently rising spur with scree conditions, running down to the water's edge. Stepping stones cross the stream and a simple path leads between the rock and planting that form a natural composition, the house and old garden wall forming an interface with the garden. This is a particularly successful rockery and the alpine plants' smallness and delicacy relate to a domestic situation very well.

Alpines need an intimate setting and a very individual style of gardening. Few people have a mountain setting to put to use, and in any case, alpines grow in the wild like gems in a grand setting.

Key to planting plan (opposite)

1. *Genista lydia*
2. *Alyssum saxatile* 'Citrinum'
3. *Pinus mugo* 'Mops'
4. *Sedum spathulifolium* 'Casablanca'
5. *Thymus citriodorus* 'Silver Posie'
6. *Soldanella montana* 'Villosa'
7. *Thymus doerfleri* 'Bressingham'
8. *Mertensia echioides*
9. *Pratia pedunculata*
10. *Omphalodes cappadocica*
11. *Veronica rupestris*
12. *Zauschneria microphylla*
13. *Campanula* 'Birch Hybrid'
14. *Astilbe simplificolia* 'Bronze Elegance'
15. *Helianthemum* 'Raspberry Ripple'
16. *Campanula carpatica* 'Chewton Joy'
17. *Silene schafta*
18. *Genista pilosa*
19. *Dodecatheon meadia*
20. *Picea glauca* 'Albertiana Conica'
21. *Oxalis adenophylla*
22. *Nierembergia rivularis*
23. *Pulsatilla vulgaris*

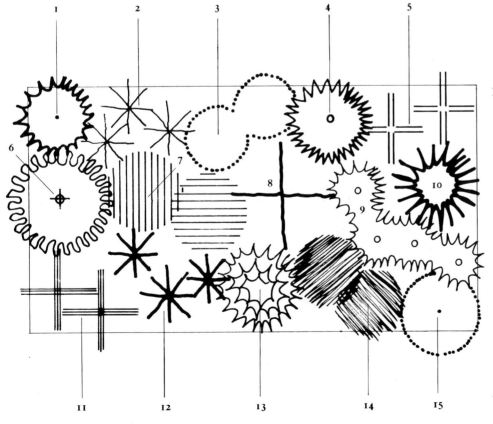

Key to planting plan

1. *Hyssopus ariastatus*
2. *Dianthus deltoides* 'Brighteyes'
3. *Saxifraga* 'Mossy Triumph'
4. *Veronica teucrium* 'Shirley Blue'
5. *Penstemon virens*
6. *Iberis* 'Snowflake'
7. *Iris setosa* 'Nana'
8. *Dodecatheon meadia*
9. *Armeria* 'Schmidtii Nana'
10. *Geranium dalmaticum*
11. *Helianthemum* 'Firedragon'
12. *Leontopodium alpinum*
13. *Phlox subulata* 'White Delight'
14. *Saxifraga* 'Elizabethae'
15. *Saponaria ocymoides*

Planting in a sink or raised bed can bring such delicate flower and foliage a little closer to eye level. Again be conscious that some species grow faster than others and may well need thinning or replacement

Easy Maintenance

In my first book on garden design I said that there were a number of basic rules to consider when planning a layout. A certain reviewer, although kind, felt that this was not the case at all but that designers created their effects through spontaneity. Anybody that knows anything about design knows how untrue this is. There are basic rules governing form, space and relationships. There are others of a more practical kind. The most important of them – and one that dictates each person's attitude to gardening – is simply this: a garden should require only as much work as the gardener is prepared to do. In other words, no one should become a slave, but have time to enjoy the 'outside room'. This does not, of course, preclude a keen gardener from spending many hours of pleasure in work, but neither does it mean that anyone with a hectic life and little interest in looking after plants is burdened by what they consider a chore.

The trend in recent years has been towards ease of maintenance, as the great increase in popularity of groundcover plants in particular bears witness. However, it is useless simply to tell people to use this type of planting. Which varieties are suitable? Are some more invasive than others? Do they flower? Of course, although we automatically think of plants as providing ground cover, this need not be the case at all. Groundcover is exactly what it says and can take the form of loose chippings, paving, grass or timber. In fact one of the best and easily maintained surfaces is a lawn, made up of many thousands of individual plants. Nobody would think of planting grass too thinly, nor should we use the more obvious groundcovers in a similar way.

Not all groundcover is particularly low growing. Little groundcover survives under mature rhododendrons and the floor of beech woodland is virtually bare. In most gardens, however, the species grown are prostrate or semi-prostrate, heathers being a particularly good example. Another recent trend is to use conifers in conjunction with heathers and some fascinating uses of these largely evergreen trees are illustrated here.

The matter of maintenance brings plants and planting immediately to mind. It is, however, quite possible to create the most attractive composition with little, if any, vegetation. As an architectural designer I can see the attraction of this. Some people would argue that it is not 'gardening' at all, in the conventional sense; however, gardens in the Japanese or Chinese style, with their economy of line and brilliant simplicity, put the matter of what gardening is into perspective. They are not 'architectural' as such: the style is a Western one, strong yet sympathetic to the adjoining house and its immediate surroundings.

This is one of the most interesting topics in the book, and in many ways closely bound up with both contemporary and future garden styles.

A green mantle of ground cover that reduces maintenance to a minimum

Groundcover

The first thing to be said about groundcover is that it is not the cure for all gardening ills. In recent years it has been suggested that this is the case, and although a carpet of foliage can certainly reduce maintenance, it can also lead to problems on its own account. Ground elder is the most superb groundcover, and has pretty seed heads too, but in the average domestic plot it would quickly run riot over everything, including the neighbours! There is, however, an attractive golden form, found in American catalogues that is slightly less rampant, although still strong. Many groundcovers are what one might normally classify as weeds, a weed being defined simply as a plant growing in the wrong place. *Hypericum calycinum* is just such a plant, thriving on hot sunny banks, with its attractive buttercup flowers. Kept in check, or allowed free rein over a space with definite boundaries, it is ideal; elsewhere it is a pest.

Why is there such interest in groundcover plants and is it leading to any particular style or in any particular direction? As the introduction to this

Key to planting plan

1 *Pachysandra terminalis*
2 *Sarcococca humilis*
3 *Ajuga reptans* 'Variegata'
4 *Bergenia cordifolia* 'Purpurea'
5 *Skimmia japonica* 'Rubella'
6 *Epimedium pinnatum* 'Colchicum'
7 *Helleborus foetidus*

The secret of using groundcover is to be bold. Drifts have to be used to be effective and here groups of 15 or 20 of a species can grow together to form a real carpet

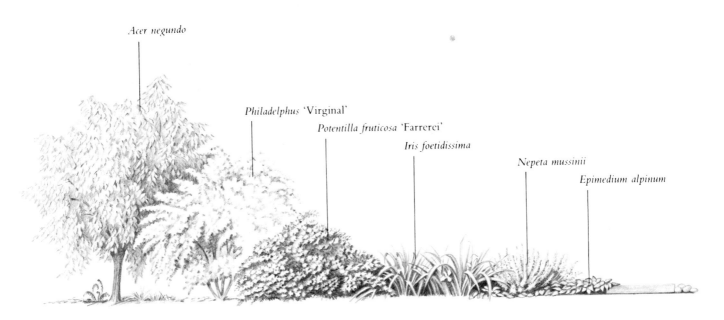

Acer negundo

Philadelphus 'Virginal'

Potentilla fruticosa 'Farrerei'

Iris foetidissima

Nepeta mussinii

Epimedium alpinum

In a natural situation, of which oak woodland is a good example, plants grow in a vertical sequence. Highest are trees, followed by shrubs and finally groundcover

chapter has said, the groundcover trend stems from ease of maintenance and the fact that there is less time available to spend in the garden. These points are, in turn, directly linked to the disappearance of the hired gardener and the reduction in garden size. There is no longer labour available for setting out yards of time-consuming bedding plants. It is enough to mow the lawn and cultivate the vegetables. In my view the boring shrub border – one or two leggy old plants surrounded by a sea of bare soil that needs continual attention to keep it clean – is not a viable proposition. There are certainly chemicals available to keep such areas clear and these can have their uses, particularly under specialist plantings such as rose beds. Purists will always have bare ground in these situations; however, I have seen hybrid tea bush roses underplanted with a variety of groundcovers, among them bulbs, which were particularly effective early in the year before the roses came into flower. One of the most successful underplantings I have seen also involved roses, but the old-fashioned shrub species. They in themselves grow fairly close to the soil but in a long border of them the foreground planting was *Hosta sieboldiana*, whose great glaucous leaves provided continuity as well as low maintenance.

Of course, many groundcovers are indiginous to the British Isles: think of ivy below trees in a woodland setting or cushions of thrift on coastal downs. The lesson to be learnt from both of these is that they flourish in specific situations. Rhododendrons, which can form excellent ground-cover, will not tolerate chalk, nor at the lower level will summer-flowering heathers. In other words, it is wise to find out what does well where.

The second golden rule has to do with continuity. There is absolutely no point in planting just one or two plants in a group: in even quite a small garden, it is advisable to plant in tens, and larger areas could well accommodate hundreds. The great Brazilian architect, Burle Marx, has evolved a style of planting in enormous sweeps of foliage and flower that use thousands of individual plants, and the effect is one of calm simplicity

Right: *Not all groundcovers need be ground hugging, a beech forest prevents virtually any undergrowth. In this garden hosta, potentilla and privet at the highest level form an effective carpet*
Below: *In light woodland or shade hosta are indispensible, particularly the variegated types that stand out against a darker background*

with the surrounding environment. The secret is to use species that can coexist without any one of them becoming invasive. In the small photograph to the right of page opposite is an excellent groundcover, epimedium, but it has been allowed to over-run the delicate little Japanese maple that is correctly planted to soften the line of the steps. If allowed to develop any further, the epimedium will quite simply choke all competition. It needs cutting back hard annuallly so that that various plants can thrive side by side. To the right azaleas form an excellent groundcover at a higher level while at the top of the steps, the distant border is edged with a low-growing juniper and *Hypericum calycinum*, which also needs a regular prune to keep it under control.

Because this type of planting is used boldly, it often relates well to an 'architectural' situation as in the larger photograph on page 115, for example. As a design I like this very much: the way in which railway sleepers form the raised beds and simple brick paving is used for the floor.

Left: *This is a very controlled use of ground cover with crisp railway sleepers framing the raised beds. Maintenance is left to a very low level with a wide range of species that complement one another*
Below: *Epimedium can be invasive, and needs cutting back hard here before it totally subdues the delicate acer*

Particularly happy is the choice of herbaceous geraniums for the groundcover, the pink foliage in the foreground adding softness to a severe ground plan. These are old-fashioned plants, the cranesbill of cottage gardens, that form a carpet of blue or pink flowers for weeks on end. Campanulas are traditional also and their white bells make their own telling statement in the middle of the border. The overall effect of this garden is to wrap one round in greenery, the use of raised beds making the most of the height of what are predominantly low-growing plants.

On the subject of architecture, I am all in favour of fostering the link between house and garden, using plants to achieve this wherever possible. One of the most unusual compositions I have seen was around a fine old Georgian lodge on a large estate. That useful standby *Cotoneaster horizontalis* was used as a definite fringe round the building, spreading both along the ground and up the walls to a height of about 1.2 m (4 ft). It looked for all the world as though the house had grown a moustache, and a handsome one at that! Once more, the success of this little composition lay in its simplicity: one species used boldly is always more successful than a surfeit of conflicting colours and textures.

To many people dead nettle, *Lamium gallobdolen*, is one of the most pernicious of plants. In the right place it is fine, being one of the few plants that will tolerate the dry, sunless conditions below trees. It thrives equally as well in the open, of course, but here its invasiveness comes to the fore. It has an attractive little flower and an equally striking leaf, an important consideration in dark places. I like it, used as it is in the smaller picture on page 118 to form a subdued carpet around a charming statue. The dark green yew hedge makes a calm back-cloth, helping to throw the figure into sharp relief.

We have been looking at groundcover used in broad sweeps but at the top of page 114 a number of species are grouped together. The underlying theme is still one of continuity and the drift of potentillas provide that. The yellow is echoed by the golden privet in the background, a plant that is a complete disaster for a hedge but ideal as a free-standing shrub, particularly in dry shade. At the opposite end of the scale, the hostas with their glaucous colour provide stability, the fat leaves a direct contrast with the busier potentillas.

An even more flamboyant note is struck in the top picture on page 118. Here is the old favourite lamium towards the front, this time in full flower. Aliums take up the middle distance while laburnum, with a hint of wisteria, looks after the roof. This is all a bit hectic for me, although the sunlight filtering through the laburnums is certainly striking. This is a restless composition but it is also spectacular and it does require very little maintenance. Gardens are full of these dilemmas – even when they are inspirational!

In the majority of cases, groundcover will take the form of shrubs or herbacious material with the bonus, if they are correctly planted, of low maintenance. Annual displays also create a carpet of colour that has its

Key to planting plan

1   3 *Euphorbia wulfenii*
2   1 *Ligustrum ovalifolium* 'Aureum'
3   6 *Veronica spicata* 'Barcarolle'
4   4 *Hosta sieboldiana*
5   4 *Potentilla* 'Elizabeth'
6   6 *Aster novii-belgii* 'Little Pink Beauty'
7   6 *Filipendula hexapetala* 'Grandiflora'

This is the planting plan of the illustration at the bottom of page 114 and shows how drifts rather than individual specimens are used to good effect

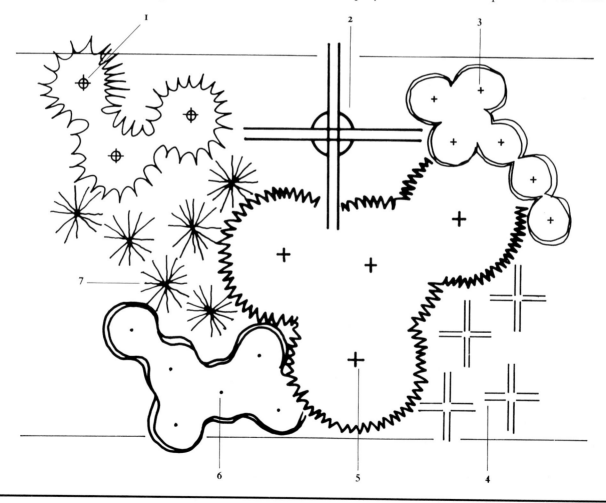

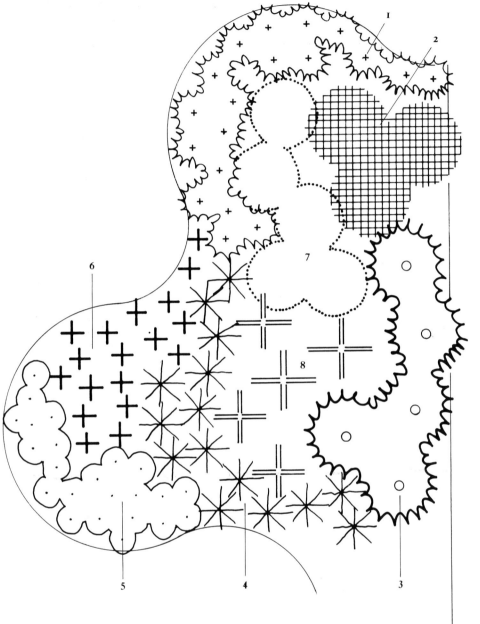

Key to planting plan

1 *Molinia caerulea* 'Variegata'
2 *Arundo donax*
3 *Miscanthus sacchariflorus*
4 *Avena candida*
5 *Festuca scoparia*
6 *Festuca glauca*
7 *Cortaderia selloana* 'Gold Band'
8 *Miscanthus sinensis* 'Purpureus'

Sensible planning so often starts on the drawing board and here one can work out not just the juxtaposition of species but the numbers required. By doing this one removes the guess work that can waste so many seasons in the garden itself

own merits. Bulbs in particular can provide interest at a time of the year when encouragement is rarely needed. The delight in coming upon a drift of winter aconites or snowdrops bring spring nearer. The vigour of a great sweep – a sweep, not a miserable scattering – of King Alfred daffodils does indeed herald a new season. Summer bedding, too – although I prefer the term summer flowers – can fill a developing shrubbery with much-needed colour. It does not need to be brash in the old parks tradition: subtle tints can transform a dull situation.

The use of grass as a groundcover was discussed earlier (see page 85), but more traditionally lawns were often planted with chamomile, that favourite herb that makes a dubious cup of tea. It is low-growing, needs no cutting and is exceptionally fragrant when crushed. Two other grasses

Lamium, or dead nettle, can be a pest in the open border, but in both these photographs it does its job to perfection. The top illustration is gaudy but practical, the one above simple and subtle; I could live with the latter but feel nervous of the former!

are also ideal, *Festuca glauca* and *Festuca scoparius*, both forming low hummocks that knit together to create a carpet.

Even grand floral displays are groundcover. I once had the dubious honour of designing the largest floral clock in England, and I have to confess that the whole thing was a ghastly mistake. It was at the time when Britain was changing from Imperial to metric measurement, and a rogue decimal point produced alarming results. As it happened, the sponsors were delighted and made much of this giant timepiece, although they never knew of the original error.

The illustration at the bottom of page 114 shows hostas again forming an effective carpet. They really are the most adaptable plants and here they are used in their favourite position, on the fringe of woodland. There are two varieties here, again used as bold swathes of contrasting green in which the variegations are reversed. Foxgloves and ferns act as a backing while rhododendrons complement the composition at a higher level before giving way to woodland trees.

A good set piece is illustrated on page 110. This, to my mind, is an excellent example of how architecture can be blended into the most natural setting. Under normal circumstances that clinical grey brick wall, with its crisp coping, would look out of place in anything but the most formal situation. Here, however, echoed by the paving, it injects an air of brightness into a woodland that, although soft in its character, is also dark.

On the floor the white flowers continue the theme while the unobtrusive vertical timber fence allows the more distant trees to be drawn quietly into the composition, without the disruption of a solid screen.

Conifers

Few conifers are indigenous to the British Isles, but there is no doubt that they are becoming increasingly popular as garden plants. To be effective they have to be used carefully: they dominate the visual field and this almost invariably makes them a focal point.

In the larger landscape, taller growing species can form a landmark many miles away. A transparency taken at Stourhead in Wiltshire which I use regularly in one of my lectures shows this perfectly. Smaller plants do exactly the same thing in a more intimate setting and this is why they need careful handling if the garden is not to become a confused jumble of unrelated features.

The problem is, of course, that many people do not fully understand the visual merits of using drifts of plants rather than individual specimens. A small garden can be very successfully planted entirely with larger and smaller conifers. They are virtually all evergreen, have a stunning variety of colour and form, once established need little maintenance in themselves, and do away with underlying infestation by weeds almost completely. They can, in addition, associate particularly well with other kinds of planting. Heathers are one example, with their own small need of maintenance and their colour throughout the year, and so, too, are other kinds of groundcover. Some of the grasses are particularly useful in this

While this is a conifer garden it also offers remarkably low maintenance. This is largely due to the use of loose cobbles, that provide the perfect foil to the striking foliage patterns

Key to planting plan

1 *Cedrus deodara*
2 *Picea pungens* 'Globosa'
3 *Erica herbacea* 'Foxhollow'
4 *Calluna vulgaris* 'Kinlochruel'
5 *Potentilla fruticosa* 'Red Ace'

There is no doubt that heathers and conifers associate remarkably well. This is the plan of the composition shown on page 122. To me the most telling statement is made by the potentillas in the middle of the group, an unexpected change of pace

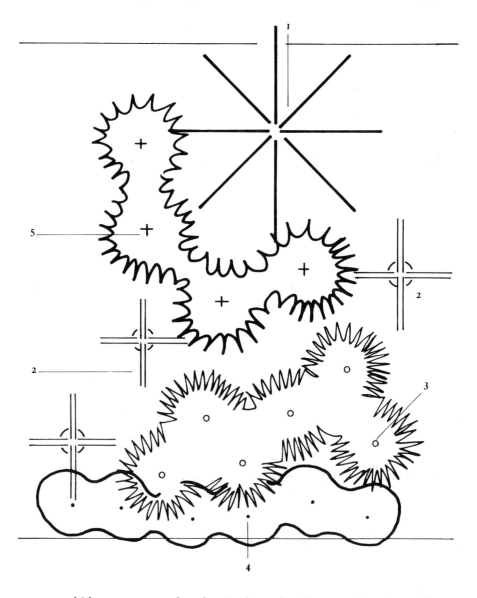

respect and I know one garden that is planted with a combination of low-growing festucas, medium-sized grasses such as avena, and the taller bamboos. Amongst these, conifers were positioned with great skill to produce a quite stunning, year-round display. In essence the success here was again due to that prime rule of design continuity: the grasses provided an undemonstrative but interesting background, with the conifers just 'lifting' the pattern and creating excitement.

I use conifers carefully, particularly the upright types. The ground-hugging junipers are indispensible, however, and a plant such as *Cedrus deodara* 'Golden Horizon', arching its branches over a raised bed or retaining wall, or set against a more upright form of, say, *Picea glauca* 'Albertiana' is excellent for planting designs.

Conifers are simply plants that produce cones and although most are evergreen some, such as larch and swamp cypress, are deciduous. In fact the deciduous group have great charm, carrying particularly beautiful spring and autumn foliage. In a larch plantation in early winter the carpet

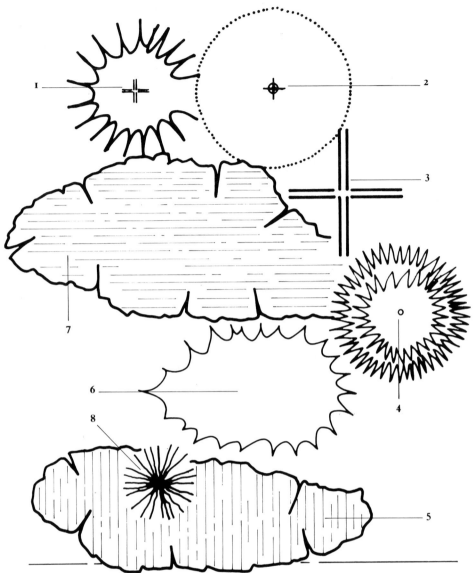

Key to planting plan

1   *Cedrus deodara*
2   *Cupressus macrocarpa* 'Aurea'
3   *Cupressus glabra*
4   *Thuja orientalis* 'Elegantissima'
5   *Juniperus horizontalis* 'Glauca'
6   *Juniperus × media* 'Old Gold'
7   *Juniperus virginiana* 'Grey Owl'
8   *Chamaecyparis* sp.

The larger conifers pictured on page 123 are shown in plan form here. This really is a design for the larger garden and underlines the point that many such plants grow to great size in a short period of time

of needles softens the footfall to a whisper.

Many conifers, including larch and swamp cypress, are forest trees, easily topping 30 m (100 ft) after not too many years. They are therefore not ideal for a small garden. The true dwarfs are the exact opposite and may only reach 0.9 m (3 ft) after more than 100 years. More often than not, however, a nursery or garden centre will sell plants whose eventual size will be between 3 and 4.5 m (10 and 15 ft), depending on variety.

Buying conifers is a question of commonsense. They are becoming slightly cheaper but they are still relatively expensive plants, simply because a lot of work is involved in bringing them to a saleable condition. The stages in this include taking cuttings or seeds, propagation, potting on, irrigation, standing out, and there are, of course, losses due to weather and other factors. Nursery land, although intensively used, carries many overheads and a plant is worth every penny paid for it. When it is seen as something appreciating in value, that may well give pleasure to future generations, the whole process comes into perspective. Another warning when buying conifers is their size, particularly the more rampant varieties. Large conifers are both expensive and transplant badly. Far better to buy a smaller more vigorous plant that will soon grow and quickly overtake a larger, more moribund specimen.

The point that heathers and other groundcovers provide an ideal foil for conifers is illustrated on page 119. This is a fine collection and one of the reasons that it is so successful is that the plants can be studied in isolation. One of the problems of a tightly planted garden is simply that there is too much going on, particularly for the specialist, who wishes to see the form and beauty of each plant. I particularly like the use of loose stones, because this neutral, almost uniform background sets off the greens and glaucous foliage perfectly. Apart from its one deciduous tree, this whole garden is planted with conifers and has a remarkable diversity of species.

There are a couple of other design elements that add to the overall success of the composition. First the lawn has been left uncluttered, as a calm, continuous sweep of grass; so often conifer enthusiasts set an assorted collection at random in the lawn itself, and the problem is made worse by the fact that each plant is surrounded by a circle of bare earth. A conifer garden is complicated, and if it is to succeed, it needs the underlying stability of grass or another medium. The second detail that I like is that simple mowing edge. Stone setts flank the lawn, reducing maintenance and adding crispness to the bed of cobbles.

The illustration below uses heathers as a groundcover, and very successfully, too. Summer-flowing heathers demand an acid soil, but the winter-flowering carnea and darlyensis varieties are far more tolerant of neutral or slightly alkaline conditions. In this setting I particularly like the colour combinations. White in the foreground is a natural lead through to the grey/blue of the conifers, which in turn make a link with the superb

Low maintenance is quite obviously a factor of the garden shown here, and is suitable for the more intimate setting

This garden is situated in the South of France and shows what can be done with conifers on a large scale

cedar in the background. Even more telling is the gold-leafed heather that runs in a 'river' between the upright conifers which act as 'islands'. The use of a potentilla at the head of the 'river' is an unlikely but successful choice, underlining the point that a species normally alien to this sort of environment can provide a useful foil. In this case it is the flower colour that links so well with the lower groundcover. Maintenance is obviously at an exceptionally low level here: the plants are so close to the surface that weeds would find a foothold almost impossible.

As far as soil and general location in the garden are concerned, most conifers are adaptable. A few, such as *Chamaecyparis pisifera*, are lime haters but yew and junipers thrive on chalk and can be seen growing wild in the countryside. Young conifers can be 'burnt' by strong, cold, winter winds, so any choice varieties would benefit from a simple screen made from hessian or fine-gauge plastic mesh. Position, too, can be important: nearly all enjoy an open, sunny aspect, particularly the golden types for whose colour sun is essential. In addition, conifers enjoy a reasonably

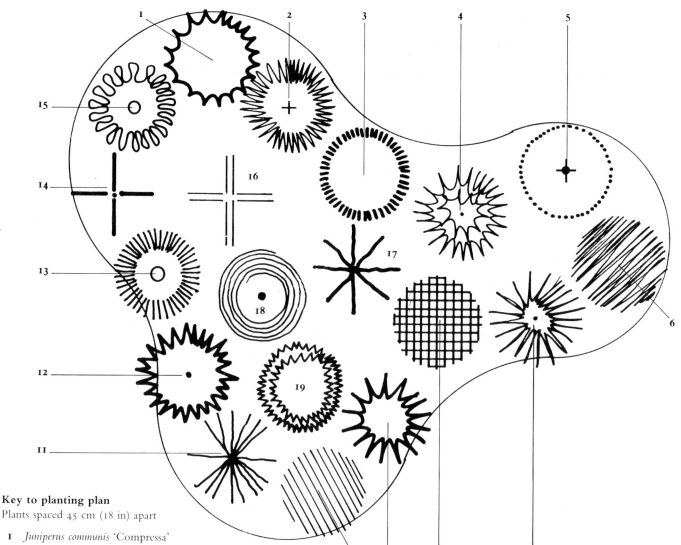

Key to planting plan
Plants spaced 45 cm (18 in) apart

1 *Juniperus communis* 'Compressa'
2 *Chamaecyparis lawsoniana* 'Pygmaea Argentea'
3 *Picea glauca* 'Albertiana Conica'
4 *Thuja orientalis* 'Aurea Nana'
5 *Thuja plicata* 'Rogersii'
6 *Juniperus squamata* 'Blue Star'
7 *Chamaecyparis pisifera* 'Nana'
8 *Thuja occidentalis* 'Rheingold'
9 *Chamaecyparis obtusa* 'Nana Lutea'
10 *Thuja occidentalis* 'Danica'
11 *Chamaecyparis pisifera* 'Boulevard'
12 *Chamaecyparis lawsoniana* 'Minima Glauca'
13 *Chamaecyparis pisifera* 'Nana Aureovariegata'
14 *Picea pungens* 'Glauca'
15 *Abies balsamea* 'Hudsonia'
16 *Cryptomeria japonica* 'Vilmoriniana'
17 *Chamaecyparis lawsoniana* 'Green Globe'
18 *Chamaecyparis pisifera* 'Filifera Aurea'
19 *Chamaecyparis lawsoniana* 'Minima Aurea'

If you are going to grow miniature conifers you are well advised to do so in a collection. Here one can see the contrasting forms without introducing a 'spotty' look to the garden as a whole

moist root run, so a soil conditioner such as peat will act as both a mulch and a moisture retainer. The annoying habit that conifers have of going bare around the base is almost invariably due to lack of water, particularly in that vital first season. Pests and diseases are remarkably few although red spider mite can be a problem on the smaller spruce, *Picea glauca* 'Albertiana', as well as in juniper and chamaecyparis varieties. A systemic insecticide used during the summer should eradicate the problem.

The dwarf, low-growing conifers lend themselves to the limited space of a domestic garden, but if room is available, the larger scale trees can be most dramatic. Few of them are indigenous to Britain except the superb *Pinus sylvestris*. The picture on page 123 is set in Nantes in France and goes to prove how successful conifers can be in a grander setting. Juniper, cedar and chamaecyparis varieties combine to form a composition that is maintenance-free and covers many square yards.

At the beginning of this section I said that conifers can become the punctuation marks of a garden or a landscape. Used with care they can fulfil a wide range of requirements; used carelessly, they are a disaster.

Architectural Gardens

The trouble with putting labels on a particular style or mood of garden is that it often gives rise to preconcieved ideas of the finished composition. So it is with the term 'architectural'. The term 'landscape architect' is vague, covering such a wide range of work, from the shaping of vast areas of countryside down to designing a tiny courtyard.

A garden in the architectural style is usually one that reflects the mood of the surrounding buildings, or is at least based on a design that relies on strength of purpose or line. It is not a modern whim: the earliest gardens were strongly architectural; the Egyptian, Persian and Moorish styles related to the buildings that adjoined them. So, too, did the Roman atrium and the Elizabethan knot. In fact, the influence of houses and a positive style is far stronger in garden history than that of the more relaxed and informal 'landscape' school. The latter was romantic, creating backdrops rather than foils to buildings. Since its time, there has been a deterioration in design, to a point where many gardens have become a watered-down travesty of their genuinely fine ancestors.

The section on patios and terraces showed how certain influences in design, from the West coast of America and Scandinavia in particular, have acted as a catalyst, producing a contemporary school of English

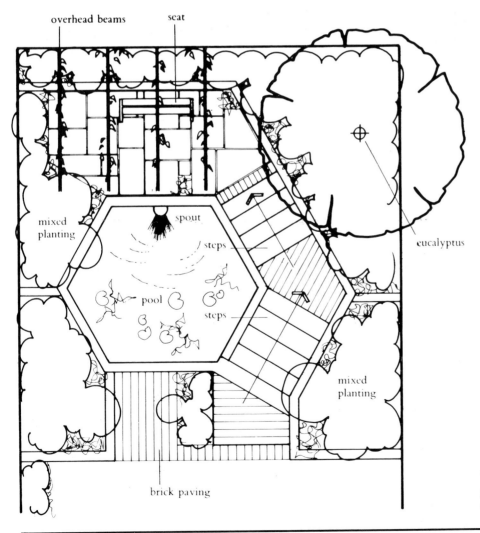

This garden looks better in reality than it does on plan. I find it all a bit restless but the planting does a great deal to pull it all together

The plan of this garden is seen on the preceding page and it is certainly architectural. The whole theme revolves around the central pool and the changes in level are cleverly handled to provide a progression through the space

Opposite: *Although this garden has been photographed just after completion you can see that the strength of line is quite superb. Once the foliage has taken hold this will be transformed into a perfect outdoor room*

garden design. It is this now thriving body that is building a whole new set of traditions, many of them strongly architectural, but that does at the same time draw on the historical connections. This weaves a unique softness into the pattern that is linked to Britain's temperate climate and to its light.

The diminishing size of gardens makes subtlety increasingly important, to allow for the maximum range of activities but also to disguise pressing boundaries that threaten to dominate these outside rooms. Boundaries are the main prerequisite of an architectural garden. They act both as a frame and a starting point for the pattern, being linked to the house and, it is hoped, compatible with it.

It is surprising just how important walls and fences are. It is also surprising how little thought is given to them in terms of suitability for a given location. If we assume that a courtyard can form a walled garden then it would be a fair bet that 70 per cent of contemporary gardens built along these lines would contain at least some of those frightful screen block walls. These are supposed to look Spanish or Mediterranian – but don't. They look stark in winter and garish in summer. Use a good old-fashioned honeycomb brick wall if you have to do anything along these lines.

In the majority of cases it comes back to simplicity, a concrete block wall, colour-washed with a neat brick-on-edge coping, works far better than a simulated stone, and costs a fraction of the price.

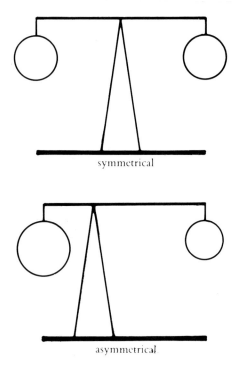

symmetrical

asymmetrical

Above: *Asymmetry simply means that you can achieve balance without regularity. At the top, two similar weights need to be equally placed either side of a fulchrum. At the bottom the weights are different, but by adjusting their position they still balance*
Right: *Abstract patterns, often taken from paintings or fabric design, can be easily translated into the ground plan of a garden. This could be the basis of lawns, water and planting, divided by any one of a range of hard surfaces*

The gardens at Versailles are architectural, but Versailles was built as a parade ground for court finery and quite literally needed an army of gardeners to keep it in condition. Today's gardens are lucky to get any kind of paid help at all, yet they have to provide shelter, seclusion and, above all, a haven from an increasingly hostile environment.

The majority of gardens in this section have been created by *my* friends and colleagues; all are contemporary and all except one are British. They make the most use of very limited space and also provide an insight into some of the brightest minds at work creating gardens today.

The non-British garden, chosen for its originality and simplicity, is actually part of a garden in Williamsburg, Virginia. It is shown on the top left of page 134. There are three basic elements here: grass, the bulb planting and finally the old tree that acts as a pivot. Each of these elements is used in such a way as to complement its neighbours but at the same time remain unobtrusive. The tree is, of course, the key to it all. A real piece of sculpture this, the old, twisted trunk and gnarled bark taking on a life of their own. It is a tree out of a fairy tale, of the kind that line dark country lanes on a winter's night and are portrayed so well by artists such as Arthur Rackham. The point here is that it is not centrally placed but offset within

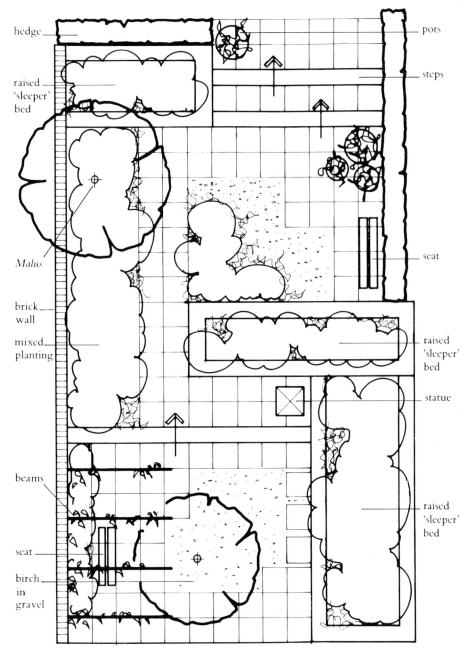

hedge

raised
'sleeper'
bed

Malus

brick
wall

mixed
planting

beams

seat

birch
in
gravel

pots

steps

seat

raised
'sleeper'
bed

statue

raised
'sleeper'
bed

This is the plan of the garden shown on page 131 and was built at Syon Park, near London, some years ago. It uses railway sleepers for steps and raised beds; the planting softens what is a severe but delightful composition

the circle, forming an asymmetric rather than a formal composition. This gives the whole design movement, the grass mown in a circular pattern emphasizing this even more. In many ways it is reminiscent of a classical Japanese garden, where sand is swept around a rock in imitation of a watercourse. Bulbs – in this case, pale yellow tulips – are the perfect foil for green grass, and the designer has had the courage to plant a single variety, producing continuity rather than the 'spotty' effect so often seen. When the bulbs die down they can be replaced by summer bedding. Here there is good reason for using such plants: they reinforce rather than detract from the picture, producing the instant colour that is so important here. A final point to notice, although they are slightly outside the immediate pattern, are the fine, old, clipped hedges. By rounding the edges they too help to reflect the theme, and the white seat nestling in one of the bays looks right, and comfortable.

Pattern is essential not only to architectural gardens but to design of all kinds, including the design of fabrics, wallpaper or carpet. All these forms of design can be translated to ground plans of gardens and the results are remarkably successful. So, too, can the work of such artists as Mondrian, whose superb geometric compositions can be an ideal starting-point for landscape design. The illustration on page 133 shows how blocks of colour and line can be substituted for paving, grass, planting and water. The key to this kind of work is, once again, asymmetry, one side or section of a design balancing another, but not by the use of equal volumes. The best way to think of this is to imagine a pair of scales with the pivot or fulchrum offset: for the two sides to balance one weight will have to be heavier than the other.

John Brookes is one of Britain's most talented designers and I was lucky enough to work with him my first job while I was still at college. The

So often the front door is forgotten but it is worth remembering that first impressions count. This is a sensitive yet practical solution to an awkward change of level

picture opposite shows a door and step arrangement at his own house. This is sheer poetry to a landscape designer and an all-important lesson in simplicity and control. It also underlines the vital point that the garden has to cater for the ugly as well as the beautiful: the raised brick area to the left houses dustbins. Brick is an obvious choice for the bin store and step risers, providing a visual link with the building. Flint is an inherently 'busy' material, so a strong foil is necessary to tone this down. The fig is ideal, its bold foliage helping to balance the store on the other side of the steps. The fig is one of my favourite plants: it grows quickly and with its great hand-shaped leaves forms a living sculpture. Planting apart from that is understated and cool, white flowers with green and grey foliage. The one high-spot is the splash of red that picks up the warmer tints of brickwork and just 'lifts' the design without being brash. As a final touch, gravel has been used for the floor: it tones well with the Cotswold paving and is cheap, no-nonsense material, quick and easy to lay.

On a very different level the garden shown on page 126 is equally successful. This is a city courtyard with very little available space, and an abrupt change of level linking two areas of the adjoining house. The problem is really one of circulation, and the pool is the key to this, acting as a pivot to the whole design. Circles can be hard to handle in a confined rectangular space, but in order to achieve a feeling of movement the designer here has bent the steps and retaining walls to lead the eye away from those dominant boundaries. Brick is sensibly used for virtually all the components and it is a material that can accommodate changing angles

Overhead beams, built from sawn-down railway sleepers, cast dappled shade on a combination of neat precast slabs and gravel

and directions because of its small modular size.

Planting is, of course, vital in such an architectural garden, particularly climbers, and although this is still a comparatively young garden, flower and foliage have gone a long way to making it an oasis. On the upper level, the white overhead beams form a canopy over the sunny sitting area and here, too, climbers are being trained to produce a green mantle. As in most compositions there is the odd discord – the use of hexagonal paving in the foreground. I would have been happier seeing either a continuation of brick or a straightforward rectangular slab that might have linked slightly better with the house.

As a final touch there is the simple fountain jet, no vast arching spray, just the sound of water on a hot, dusty, city day.

One of the best, and to my mind underrated, designers in England today is Victor Shanley. One of his many gardens is shown on page 127, and it is typical of his brisk, uncluttered style. Here, again, there is limited space and brick paving is used as the main floor material. It is interesting that this is such a popular surface among designers. It is adaptable, links well with an adjoining wall or house and has at the same time that mellowness that gives an outside room maturity. In the illustration the floor has a slightly unusual basket weave pattern that uses three bricks instead of the usual four. Split level pools are wrapped around two sides of the terrace, water being recirculated by a submersible pump. Timber is the ideal foil for brick and the dark solid planks cross the water in two directions. The fence echoes the theme in the vertical plane, the slender cedar boards having a much lighter feel as they reach upwards. I particularly like the niche created for the statue, and the bold palm that forms a striking contrast to both paving and fence.

Gravel is used as a secondary surface, railway sleepers continuing the timber theme, leading both feet and eye back to the brick path. One of the most imporant things about this design is that it is still in its youth, the planting having yet to develop. It does, however, stand by its strength of line, an absolutely vital prerequisite for any garden. Once softened by foliage, it will go on improving – unlike many designs that degenerate into a visual mess through the addition of plants.

Some years ago, at Syon Park, near London, a unique gardening exhibition was born. It covered many acres and was set within the confines of an original Capability Brown landscape. It set out not only to create a living dictionary of plants but to cover everything to do with gardening, including tools, equipment, garden buildings and free advice. Unfortunately, due to management difficulties it closed some five years later. It was a unique and inspiring event. I started my design career there. It contained many 'individual gardens', one of which is shown on page 131. This was affectionately called the 'sleeper' garden and was largely built of those massive but useful lengths of timber. It was a simple composition floored with a combination of neat precast slabs and gravel, the pale colour of the latter forming a sharp contrast to the dark sleepers. This photograph looks through the overhead beams to catch a glimpse of

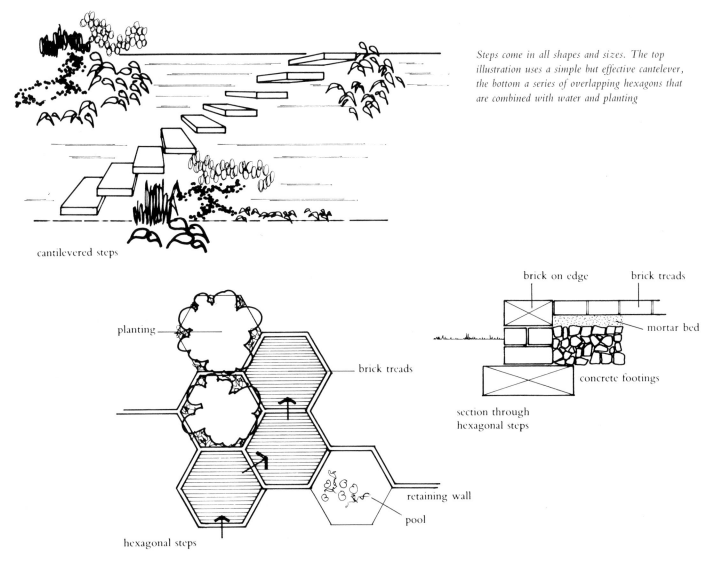

cantilevered steps

*Steps come in all shapes and sizes. The top
illustration uses a simple but effective cantelever,
the bottom a series of overlapping hexagons that
are combined with water and planting*

planting

brick treads

hexagonal steps

retaining wall

pool

brick on edge   brick treads

mortar bed

concrete footings

section through
hexagonal steps

Flora, the horticulturalists' goddess, in the far distance. Russian vine, that
most rampant of climbers, covers the beams. I must admit, that I am really
rather fond of this hooligan of climbers. All it needs is a strong arm and a
pair of shears to keep it happily in check. The garden is built on a slight
slope, emphasizing the clever use of raised beds, and the sleepers form
broad and practical steps.

That last garden was built by a successful firm of nurserymen. The next
at the top right of page 134, is by David Hicks, better known for his
sophisticated interiors. It is in many ways an unusual piece, breaking some
of the more conventional rules of garden design. However, no rules are
sacrosanct and if a designer is clever – and Mr. Hicks most certainly is –
you can get away with it! In essence this is a long, narrow space which
many people would have broken up into 'individual rooms', detracting
from the length that creates both surprise and suspense. Here we have the
exact opposite, all the elements combining to emphasize the distant view.
On either side lime trees, which could later be pleached, echo the walls and
lead the eye towards the austere obelisk. Beneath the trees is planted a
single species of herbaceous geranium, *Geranium endresii*, a good
groundcover and ideal in shady conditions. York stone acts as an

Above: *This American garden uses concentric rings of tulips around an old tree which is in itself a piece of sculpture*
Right: *A simple and measured statement that emphasises the length of this narrow garden. It cuts across the obvious design rule of subdivision, but is the more effective for it*
Below: *Beautifully laid slates echo the bold circle of granite setts and planting*

undemonstrative floor and the pink geraniums are cleverly complemented by the blue and white tablecloth.

This really is purist design. In totally practical terms it would be exceptionally drab (or dramatic) in winter, with no leaves or flowers, just paving, walls and branches to hold it together. It is, however, inspirational in the best sense. I like it very much.

The final picture, at bottom left of this page is a detail of part of the conifer garden illustrated on page 119. It really emphasizes that although the broad spread of an architectural garden needs to be elegantly handled, so too do those small, intimate corners. All the materials, here are natural old stone walls, granite setts, a charming yet traditional technique of setting slates on edge. The latter fan out from the bold leaves of bergenia and, being thin, conform to the circular pattern exactly. This is a composition that will hold its interest throughout the year, in many ways the test of any architectural garden.

This section is purposely one of the longest in the book because the gardens considered in it are signifcant for the direction which contemporary landscape design is taking. It is true that there is a great diversity of style here, but this simply underlines the point that the design movement is in good heart.

Inspiration consists of a rightness for a particular purpose. All these gardens achieve this rightness by not only sitting comfortably in their particular environment but also serving the people for whom they were built. They are the ideal outdoor room, and that is what gardening is all about.

Gardens without Plants

There are, in fact, remarkably few gardens entirely without plants and it could well be argued that a garden would not be a garden without them. There are, however, situations in which planting is kept to an absolute minimum. This might be for a variety of reasons, one of which could well be inhospitable conditions, including a lack of soil or a particularly harsh climate. In addition, certain styles of garden can be weighted more towards hard landscape than soft. The book looks a little later on at Japanese and Chinese gardens, both of which can look austere to Western eyes until it is understood that a particular surface – say, gravel, sand or loose stones – is used to imitate water in a natural setting. This may be highlighted by a single group or an individual plant, representing a forest or wood.

Closer to home, a terrace or patio is essentially a garden without plants and so, too, is a roof garden, although planting can be introduced to enhance all of these. Trees are the biggest plants of all, and a woodland garden relies heavily on the tracery of branches and stems rather than on the intimate character of foliage and flower. Trees can, in fact, form the basis of fascinating outside rooms: I once created a series of terraces, built from timber decking, that worked their way down a hillside from a superb modern house cantilevered out from the slope. Those decks were without conventional planting but I incorporated the stems of trees in

Above: *Grasses and stone echo a dry river bed that would only support minimal vegetation*
Left: *Brick and loose cobbles with the minimum of planting provide a sophisticated approach to this front door*

them so that they soared through the crisply detailed planks. In summer, with sunlight filtering through the canopy and casting dappled shade, this was a delightful place and very much a garden.

Water can be used as a unifying element in a garden setting in much the same way. In another contemporary house, I worked closely with the architect and built a set of pools that flowed from inside a conservatory area into an austere but beautiful courtyard. Here different levels allowed the water to slide and cascade in a never-ending circle. This, together with an intricate paving pattern, was enough to compensate for the intentional exclusion of all planting. In consequence there was no maintenance. The question is really a psychological one: are we prepared to accept that such a space is a garden? On balance I think we should.

The larger picture on page 135 is not entirely devoid of plants, but it is certainly austere. To my mind, it does not quite go far enough: there are a couple of detail points that tend to detract from the overall picture. The first is that fussy little upstand at the base of the vine that is quite unnecessary; a gap could have been left in the paving. The other jarring note are the two rocks that tend, I fear, to have a Japanese 'flavour'. Flavours are dangerous things in garden design and often indicate indecisiveness. The relationship of those stones with the rest of the composition is not quite right, and I would have left them out.

However, the overall concept really is very handsome. The clean brick walls are echoed by the paving, the loose cobbles making an attractive foil to both hard and soft landscape. The planting is well chosen, particularly

The way in which stone or man-made materials can be laid lends character to an area. Rigid patterns produce an architectural feel, informal patterns the opposite. Sometimes, as in the bottom left illustration, hard and soft landscape come together, the grass growing through specially made concrete blocks

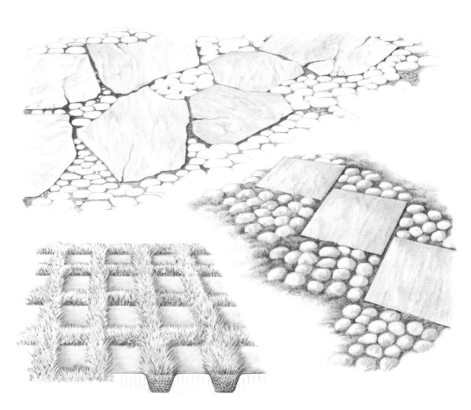

the contrast between the feathery bamboo and the great, round vine leaves, while the brass house name is mercifully simple. The step is neat, but, again, just a little contrived: a recessed riser, painted black, would have allowed it to float rather more successfully. The essence of these very architectural compositions is that the detailing has to be crisp and perfect; there is no room in them at all for compromise, otherwise they miss their point.

The second, smaller photograph is altogether softer: a stone garden in a dry river bed. Here there are interesting contrasts of leaf shape and size, made by grasses of different types, leading up to the tall bamboos in the background. This is an almost entirely evergreen display looking good at any time of the year. The stones are piled in random masses, and there is an overall floor of gravel, reducing maintenance to a minimum and also providing continuity.

As a penultimate thought, which is not as fantastic as it first sounds, I am working on a garden using fibre optics instead of plants. These thin filaments carry light to their tips and look much like grasses; illuminated from within, the result at night is thrilling. In fact it is just as thrilling as using normal outside lights.

I must admit to having an admiration for gardens before they are planted at all. The bones are laid bare for all to see and it is then that a design fault becomes obvious. Planting, of course, brings gardens to life, provides the pleasure of colour and interest throughout the year. The trouble is that I am a purist!

Symbolism is an essential part of the Japanese garden tradition. A swirling stream or angry sea can be depicted by boulders set in a pattern of raked sand or gravel

THEMES ON ONE COLOUR

Every garden has a theme, but the trouble is that some compositions have too many. To be effective a theme should be single-minded and create a definite mood, allowing the incidental furnishings to sit comfortably within the overall pattern.

The choice of theme should not only have a purpose but should also respect the immediate surroundings. There is absolutely no point in creating a Chinese garden in a obviously English setting. In fact the real point is that such an indigenous style can only look correct in its own country and the closest we should or could get is an honest interpretation. This is precisely the point of a good cartoon drawing – it simplifies and mimics the subject without slavishly copying it.

Many people would argue that their own garden has absolutely no theme at all, but if it is correctly designed then that theme is the personality of the people concerned.

One of my more bizarre clients collected totem poles from North America. His was a specialist hobby and the only place these enormous hewn timbers could be viewed was in the garden. Consequently my task was to site them in the most appropriate way, bearing in mind their strength of line and overall theme. In fact that job was both fascinating and not as difficult as would at first appear. Totem poles are simply sculpture and we arranged them in such a manner as to visually link the house and an adjoining woodland. Once in the latter we created a central clearing that housed the major part of the collection. It was a sobering experience to walk down a woodland path and happen upon the group of totems; they echoed the line of the surrounding trees in a strangely sinister way.

For our purposes we have looked towards colours and countries to provide a theme. The former is a vital ingredient in creating mood. Gardens that use red are hot and strong, while gardens using green are calm and restful. In many ways it comes back to the whole idea of treating the garden as an outdoor room. However, people who are quite adept at creating a mood indoors find it extremely difficult to extend their thinking beyond the confines of the house.

My own garden has a very positive theme and that is simply lack of work. This is not as bland as it may appear, for the use of broad-leaved ground-covering plants, many of which are predominantly green or variegated, set a very positive pattern. This architectural style of planting is echoed in the paving and other hard landscape detailing and so the prerequisite of low maintenance had a very strong bearing on the overall garden character. This approach is one of the designers main tools. Give him or her a requirement and this will be interpreted into or become a theme.

Green is the colour of the landscape, at least in temperate climates. This garden, linked with the timber chalet, is totally natural and undeniably restful

The Colours

We tend to think of colour relating only to plant material, but this is quite wrong. There are many things in a garden that are inert. Furniture, fabrics, pots and containers; the tint of a wall that runs from the inside to the open garden. It is in fact these underlying features that so often set a theme and upon which a colour scheme can be based. This is precisely where so many gardens fall down, they have little respect for the ground rules that may well dictate the dominance of a certain colour.

Green

Green can be extraordinarily restful. I find it quite the most understated yet subtle colour scheme in the garden. It is, of course, the basic theme of the landscape, not just in Britain but across the world, apart from those areas that are parched or frozen. Even there, when the weather softens, the land is often brought back to greenness by rain or thaw.

The range of green tends to be overlooked. It can vary from the pale end of the spectrum verging on yellow to the darkest leaves of, say, *Hedera colchica*, which are almost black. In between lies a wealth of subtle tints. In

Key to planting plan

1	1	*Fatsia japonica*
2	1	*Pyracantha rogersiana*
3	3	*Garrya elliptica*
4	5	*Skimmia japonica* 'Fragrans'
	2	*Skimmia japonica* 'Foremanii'
5	23	*Pachysandra terminalis*
6	4	*Helleborus corsicus*
7	2	*Mahonia lomariifolia*
8	2	*Viburnum tinus*
9	3	*Elaeagnus ebbingii*

This evergreen border is ideal for a shady situation or even a north facing wall. It would provide colour and interest throughout the year as well as effective ground cover

many ways the problem is that there is too much choice: all those catalogues and garden centres bursting with brightly coloured bedding, shrubs and herbaceous material. History is no help either, for as soon as the landscape school subsided, it was replaced by those avid plant collectors who scoured the world for bigger and better blooms. We owe a great deal to those people but the fruit of their labours does tend to complicate many otherwise simple garden problems.

A green garden is often considered a contemporary phenomenon, although most of the classic garden styles relied heavily on green. The picture on page 138 is modern: a paved courtyard, with granite setts used for the floor – these rather clinical shapes are an ideal foil for the vegetation. Planting is used in blocks of one or two species, forming a tight carpet that reduces maintenance to a minimum. There is a high proportion of evergreen material here, but the sumach, *Rhus typhina laciniata*, close to the house, has brilliant red autumn foliage, in direct contrast to the other planting, and its sculptural stems form an architectural tracery against the crisp cream brick wall and timber

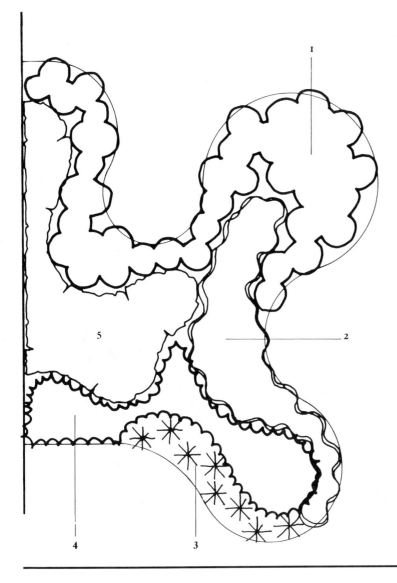

Key to planting plan

1 *Hedera helix* 'Glacier'
2 *Hedera helix* 'Caenwoodiana'
3 *Hedera helix* 'Gold Heart'
4 *Hedera helix* 'Chrysocarpa'
5 *Hedera canariensis* 'Gloire de Marengo'

An ivy collection that could be extended to cover an almost unlimited area. Like the collection on the previous page this planting would be quite happy in shade

Green is also so often the colour of the waterside, as this pretty composition bears testimony. The architectural bridge is the perfect foil for the more delicate plants

building. Many people would call this an architectural garden and indeed it is: the solid wedges of plants complement the surroundings perfectly.

A lawn is generally thought of simply as grass, but it is, of course, made up of millions of individual green plants. The gardens at Dartington Hall in Devon are built up from a superb series of grass banks and terraces. Dark green yew trees carefully placed and clipped provide emphasis while a background of woodland trees complete the picture. In the soft grey Devon light, tempered by mist, this can be a startling, an example of how a single colour can be used to maximum effect.

The next picture, above, continues the green theme, this time round a small pool in an altogether more intimate setting. The clever thing about this composition is the crisply detailed timber bridge. The boards are precisely cut to form a cleverly mitred joint, a detail that, if poorly constructed, would have ruined the whole concept. Without such a clearly defined walkway the whole garden would have become simply a jumble of assorted greenery, but the bridge prevents this from happening. The ever-popular bamboo plays a major role: it really is an adaptable plant, being equally happy in a boggy ditch or a dry bank. Marginal and groundcover plants cleverly disguise the edge of the pool, running together to form a carpet, and the foliage on the banks climbs until it finally reaches the rhododendron.

Many shade-tolerant species are not only evergreen but have green flowers, too. There is a particularly fine north-facing border at Capel Manor in Hertfordshire, well worth a visit, containing ivies, *Garrya eliptica*, hellebores and that interesting semi-climber, fatshedera, a cross

Herbaceous and therefore seasonal planting of white. Form and height are juxtapositioned to lead the eye down from the back of the border

between ivy and fatsia. Its variegated form is particularly striking and quite hardy; it has just come through a vicious winter unscathed in my own garden.

An interesting group of plants is shown on page 140. This contains all those just mentioned as well as skimmias, sarcococca, *Viburnum davidii* and *Pachysandra terminalis*, a good groundcover plant. It provides colour and interest throughout the year and, in addition, it is as tough as old boots!

Ivy has many merits. I regularly design ivy collections and the variety of leaf form and shape is enormous. Variegation makes the range of choice even greater. Rectangular interlocking patterns can link superbly with well detailed paving, while sweeps and curves look more handsome in an informal situation. In order to limit the invasiveness of these rampant groundcovers I usually insert a deep metal strip between varieties; a ruthless trim with shears once a year also keeps things in check. Ivy can easily be encouraged to run over a wire frame to form a 'fedge', to define a particular area or create a division across the garden. Ivy can also be used to form topiary figures in a fraction of the time normally taken to train a hedge.

White

Probably the best-known of all white theme gardens is Sissinghurst in Kent. Started by Vita Sackville-West in the 1930s, it now belongs to the National Trust, which probably does more than any other organization in England to preserve and improve unique gardens. The white garden at Sissinghurst is a large, restful area, with mellow brick paths that lead both

Key to planting plan

1 *Crambe cordifolia*
2 *Hydrangea serrata* 'Greyswood White'
3 *Hosta fortunei* 'Thomas Hogg'
4 *Halimiocistus × sahucii*
5 *Hibiscus syriacus* 'Totus Albus'
6 *Veronica virginica*
7 *Phlox paniculata* 'Frau A. Buchner'
8 *Hosta plantaginea*
9 *Phlox paniculata* 'White Admiral'
10 *Anemone japonica* 'Alba'
11 *Kniphofia uvaria*
12 *Hebe pinguifolia* 'Pagei'
13 *Anemone × hybrida* 'Louise Uhink'
14 *Cistus × florentinus*

In this formal composition white again plays the dominant role but with a mixture of planting that will provide interest over a considerable period

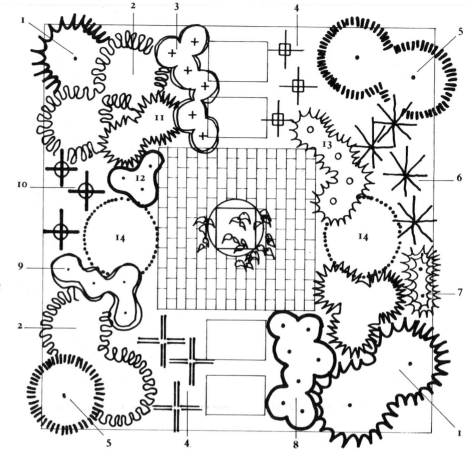

feet and eye towards a centrally placed arbour. Sissinghurst is an entire composition, but most people have room only for a single border, or even part of a border. I particularly like the photograph on page 143, for a number of reasons. For a start, the plants are used in great cloudy drifts, and they are all my particular favourites. In the foreground are those marvellous cottage garden plants, marguerite daisies that also grow wild, powdering verges and old railway cuttings. At the back spires of delphineums tower over the border and the lilies add the pleasure of their perfume. These are, of course, herbaceous, the marguerites being unable to withstand the frosts of winter.

In many ways white is the typical flower colour of the countryside, particularly in early summer, when all the parsley family are in bloom. In the garden the range of white is much greater: white Japanese anemones for valuable late flower, Canterbury bells, columbine and aruncus. Slightly more unusual are the massive *Crambe cordifolia*, the graceful spikes of cimicifuga and the beautiful arum, *Zantedeschia aethiopica* 'Crowborough', hardy enough if covered with straw in the winter. Then there are shrubs, *Philadelphus* 'Beuclerk', with its perfume, compact and ideal for the smaller garden. White floribunda and shrub roses are essential and *Magnolia stellata* 'Water Lily' is one of the finest spring plants.

The white garden at Wyards Farm, Hampshire, shown on page 146, is delightfully informal – and not all white. Sulphur-yellow sprays of the indispensible *Alchemilla mollis* flank the path that leads away from the

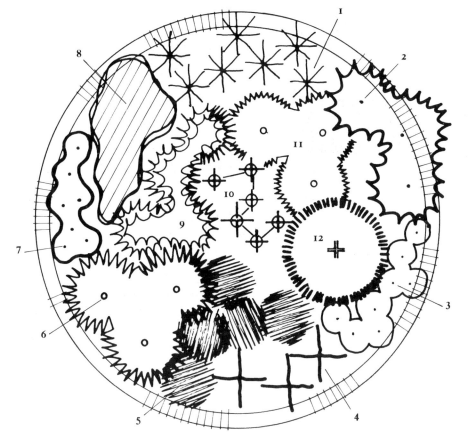

A collection of silver and grey foliage that always has a magic of its own. Not only has it a traditional quality but such a colour is the harmoniser of any garden, tying separate colour ranges together

pretty terracotta urns. Phlox is another indispensible border plant, flowering as it does relatively late in the season. The best white phlox, to my mind, is *Phlox paniculata* 'Fujuyama', an American cross that is widely available. White plants can, of course, be complemented, as they are at Wyards, by white Versailles tubs or a crisply painted white seat. The latter always provides a focal point, particularly when positioned against a dark background or under trees. An old park bench in an orchard strewn with wild flowers beside a meandering mown grass path is a heavenly spot on a hot summer day. Poppies should always be planted in rough grass to look their best: *Papaver orientalis* 'Black and White' is a gem, with pure white petals and an inky splotch at the base. The flowers are short lived but keep on coming, the foliage can be cut down in late summer when an orchard area is mown.

Pink

Pink as a flower colour tends to be just a little prissy. However, there are exceptions. Pink lies in that soft colour range of blue, purple, grey and white and as such can play an important role, heightening a distant view and blending into boundaries or landscape. The picture on page 147 works because the larger-scale iris flowers act as a foil to the delicate pink stars of the other flowers. The lesson here, once again, is continuity.

Pink is one of the better winter colours, for pale shades have more chance of making a statement against a low-key background: examples

The white garden at Wyards Farm in Hampshire is not quite all white. The sulphur yellow flowers of alchemilla just adding that often indispensible colour break

are the unexpected flowers of *Daphne mezereum*, actually indigenous to Britain, or *Viburnum grandiflorum*. On a smaller scale, many of the bergenia varieties are effective, while heathers can provide the most striking display of all. On neutral or slightly alkaline soil the carnea and darlyensis types are ideal. Pink *Erica darlyensis* 'Darly Dale' and carmine *Erica carnea* 'Vivellii', grown together in bold drifts can make a vibrant pattern on a bleak day when little else can tolerate the conditions.

During the summer the choice is virtually unlimited, but one or two of the less known species are particularly worth while. *Anemone lesseri* is a delightful hybrid with chalice-like flowers, and *Diascia rigescens*, a native of the Cape Province in South Africa, is a hardy perennial that is well worth growing. It grows up to about 45 cm (18 in) high, and has warm pink flowers right through from June to October; the soft green foliage is dense enough to act as a worthwhile summer groundcover.

Another pink bloom, and one that is under-used and under-estimated, is *Incarvillea delaveyi*. This has deep pink trumpets of flower that form a glowing pattern in any border during those hot summer months of June and July. Again the plants are only 45 cm (18 in) or so high and are therefore ideal for an underplanting towards the front of a bed, or set within a random paved area of old York stone.

The photograph at the top of page 150 is a final, softer study in pink, the great spires of foxgloves towering over the shrub roses at a lower level. Both these plants are indispensable in any garden, particularly a gently modelled country situation. They are adaptable too, the foxgloves being tolerant of shade and able to self-seed themselves everywhere, much to the annoyance of over-zealous gardeners. Shrubs roses have the old-fashioned, traditional atmosphere about them, the result of generations of

Pink and purple mixed. This wonderful combination is made up of large-flowered iris and small-leaved pinks

breeding. Not only do the majority of species have fragrant, delicate flowers but also hips, attractive foliage and arching stems, the latter providing of winter interest.

Purple

True purple is a fine, rich colour conjuring up a vision of summer and long, well-tended herbaceous borders. Purple leaves play a vital role in planting design, acting as a foil to many other colours. The purple smoke bush, *Cotinus coggygria* 'Folius Purpureis', planted beneath the gold leaves of *Robinia pseudoacacia* 'Frisia', is one of the classic combinations of planting design. On a lower level a lovely combination is *Senecio greyii* teamed with *Salvia officinalis* 'Purpurascens' or *Sedum spectabile* 'Autumn Joy'. In a larger landscape setting, copper beech is the supreme champion, some forms showing exceptionally dark purple leaves. Copper beeches show up best planted as a feature against a background of common beech, *Fagus sylvatica*, or other deciduous woodland trees. In the smaller garden

Key to planting plan

1 *Elaeagnus ebbingii*
2 *Viburnum rhytidophyllum*
3 *Prunus lusitanica*
4 *Euonymus japonica*
5 *Arundinaria nitida*
6 *Skimmia japonica*
7 *Choisya ternata*
8 *Artemesia* 'Lambrook Silver'
9 *Hebe* 'Midsummer Beauty'
10 *Hydrangea petiolaris*
11 *Garrya elliptica*
12 *Acer palmatum*
13 *Hakonechloa macra* 'Albo-aurea'
14 *Clematis macropetala*
15 *Dicentra spectabile*
16 *Hosta sieboldiana*
17 *Hosta sieboldiana*
18 *Iris* 'Jane Phillips'
19 *Vitis coignetiae*
20 *Hydrangea macrophylla* 'Blue Wave'
21 *Hebe subalpina*
22 *Cytisus* × *kewensis*
23 *Juniperus* × *media* 'Sulphur Spray'
24 *Hebe speciosa*
25 *Phormium tenax*
26 *Jasminum officinale*
27 *Santolina incana*
28 *Euphorbia wulfenii*
29 *Mahonia lomariifolia*
30 *Hydrangea serrata* 'Greyswood'
31 *Skimmia japonica* (× 2)
32 *Garrya elliptica*
33 *Aucuba japonica*
34 *Pachysandra terminalis*
35 *Hypericum calycinum*
36 *Vinca minor*
37 *Rosmarinus officinalis* 'Miss Jessop's Upright'
38 *Hosta albo* 'Picta'
39 *Lavandula angustifolia* 'Vera'
40 *Potentilla fruticosa* 'Red Ace'
41 *Senecio* 'Sunshine'
42 *Rosmarinus officinalis* 'Miss Jessop's Upright'
43 *Potentilla* 'Tangerine'
44 *Cedrus deodara* 'Golden Horizon'
45 *Hosta alba* 'Picta Aurea'
46 *Festuca scoparia*
47 *Festuca glauca*

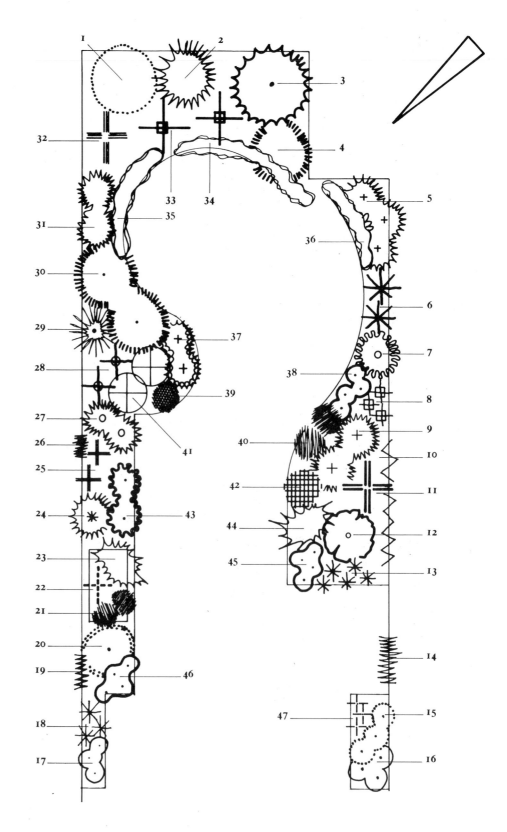

This is the planting plan for a very typical size of garden. It is planned to give maximum interest across the seasons as well as keeping maintenance to a reasonable level. Plants are grouped in drifts to provide continuity with taller, background and screening material at the periphery

Prunus pissardii is an excellent choice, particularly if there is room for two or three whitebeam in the background, the pale green leaves of the latter acting as the perfect foil.

An excellent example of the purple cotinus is used as a background plant in the smaller picture on page 150, showing why it is called the 'smoke' bush. The flowers are produced in feathery masses and go on

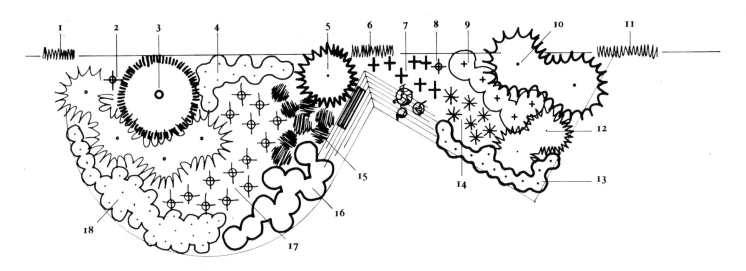

Mixed border against a south wall using purple and grey as the main components, with a dash of white to add purity. Again note how plants are used in sweeps rather than singly in isolation

throughout the summer. The great thing about purple and its direct counterpart, grey, is that they are the harmonisers of the flower border; nearly everything looks good in association with them and they have the effect of toning down the worst excesses of taste and colour. This is precisely what is being achieved by the cotinus and, to a lesser extent, the *Ricinus communis* in the middle of the picture. The latter is the old Victorian favourite, the castor oil plant, not hardy but a sculptural shape throughout the summer. In this case the purple is helping to tone down the vivid reds that would otherwise be fighting for attention. This border is somewhat alarming, if not spectacular. It underlines the point made earlier in the book, that the hot colours of the spectrum draw the eye and foreshorten space.

Red and Yellow

Roses can be planted as a solid block colour: red can be used to a stunning effect in this way. Another design idea is to mix them within a hot or cool colour range, or use them singly to create a point of emphasis. A scarlet floribunda within a larger border of soft colour can simply lift the composition or lead the eye in a particular direction. This element of the unexpected adds greatly to what might otherwise be competent but ordinary.

Yellow and red are in the same range, and although colour is usually associated with the summer months, there is a wealth of spring colour, too: yellow aconites, crocus and daffodils, followed by glowing red tulips – a procession of colour leading into the new year.

On page 153 there is a slightly unusual planting plan that relies to a great extent on leaf colour, although it includes flowers to add a little extra brightness. This is a bed of ample size, where maintenance has been kept to a minimum by the use of groundcover. At the back are the striking leaves of *Eleagnus ebbingii* 'Limelight', a far better proposition than the more traditional *Pungens maculata*. The former is a fast-growing shrub whose evergreen leaves cheer the dullest winter days. Golden privet extends the line at the back of the border and although this is a pernicious hedging plant, it is superb as a free-standing shrub, providing screening, shelter and interest.

Foxgloves really are one of the cottage garden stars and here they look quite superb against the old stone wall behind

A restless but nevertheless spectacular planting of castor oil plants, dahlias and phlox. There is perhaps room for this sort of approach in certain gardens, but it produces migraine in some of us

Kerria japonica, the old batchelor's button, is a much underrated spring-flowering shrub. One of Gertrude Jekylls favourites, still available, is the golden-leafed elder, *Sambucus racemosa* 'Plumosa Aurea'. The finely cut leaves unfold to cover a shrub of considerable size. Lower down the scale, golden rod is always a favourite; the older varieties did have faults but the new types, such as *Solidago goldeninosa*, reach about 90 cm (3 ft), in a neat compact shape, and their colour is an urgent, strong yellow, no pale compromise. Black-eyed Susan is another 'must' for flowering later in the season, the original of which is *Rudbeckia newmanii*, producing blooms from July to September.

Filipendula ulmaria 'Aurea' is another good but unusual choice, reaching a height of 45 cm (18 in), with golden-yellow leaves that are undoubtably spectacular. The flowers are insignificant but this hardy perennial forms a tight canopy of foliage that excludes weed growth. Of the groundcovers here, *Alchemilla mollis* and *Euphorbia polychroma*, the former has flowers of

Silver-foliaged plants stand out well in a planting scheme, sometimes making a useful transition between more brightly coloured plants

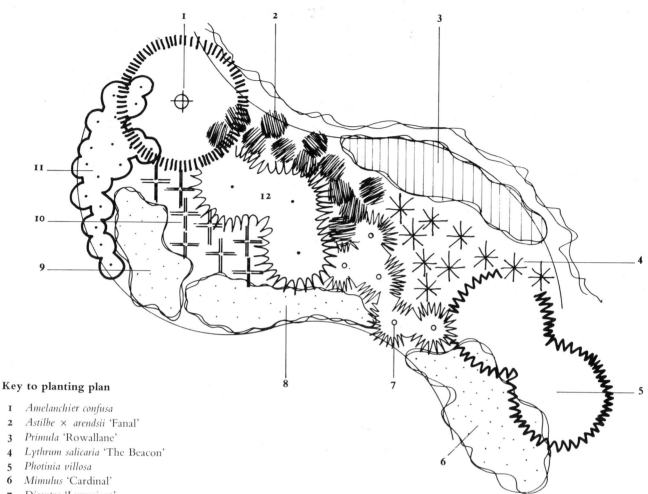

Key to planting plan

1   *Amelanchier confusa*
2   *Astilbe × arendsii* 'Fanal'
3   *Primula* 'Rowallane'
4   *Lythrum salicaria* 'The Beacon'
5   *Photinia villosa*
6   *Mimulus* 'Cardinal'
7   *Dicentra* 'Luxuriant'
8   *Polygonum milletii*
9   *Primula pulverulenta*
10 *Hemerocallis* 'Stafford'
11 *Bergenia* 'Ballawley'
12 *Cornus alba* 'Siberica'

Red really is vibrant but here it is used in all its guises, with flower, stem and foliage producing something of interest throughout the seasons

true sulphur yellow, the latter bracts of a slightly stronger colour. Both of them, when used in bold drifts, are worth their weight in gold.

Grey

Grey is the work horse in nearly every design field, whether it is furnishing, fabrics or planting. In the garden it is particularly valuable, often cropping up in those felty grey leaves that are so important in seaside conditions. Purple and grey are safe for novice and professional alike. *Veronica pinnata* 'Blue Eyes' or *Salvia superba* 'Lubeca', underplanted with a long sweep of *Hebe pinguifolia* 'Pagei', is almost too good to be true.

Many grey plants tend to be low growing, *Festuca glauca*, *Hosta sieboldiana*, *Stachys lanata* – the lambs lugs of cottage gardens – among them. In the middle of a border the sculptural line of eryngium, with its great grey teazles, is a 'must' and so, too, are the larger hebes, 'Midsummer Beauty' or 'Great Orme'. Many grey plants are also suitable for roof gardens, particularly those that have felty leaves with resistance to drying out in windy or semi-arid conditions: they include *Senecio greyii*, *Phlomis fruticosa* and genista and potentilla, with their slightly greener foliage.

On an altogether larger scale, *Salix caprea*, the sallow or goat willow, is one of Britain's finest native shrubs. If allowed to develop it becomes a small tree but most willows – and caprea is no exception – benefit from hard pruning to encourage young growth. The leaves are up to 10 cm (4 in) long and soft grey on the underside. A generous plantation sliding down to a lake margin is, indeed, nothing short of inspirational especially in overcast weather, when sky, foliage and water form a grey palette that is worked by the wind into ever-changing patterns. From the other side of the world, gum trees provide grey foliage that blends into domestic garden patterns particularly well. Many of the Australian eucalyptus are not hardy enough for the British climate but the variety *gunnii* is ideal. This has glaucous leaves that, as well as being a favourite of flower arrangers, have that well-known aromatic smell. This variety is a fast grower and forms a screen quickly without becoming dominant, and the fact that it is evergreen is another advantage. If it is damaged by frost, or if it outstrips a given situation, it may simply be cut down to ground level: it quickly regenerates and in doing so takes on an attractive shrubby appearance.

The essence of these theme gardens is not monotony but variety. A picture created in a single colour is far from uninteresting. In many ways it expresses a basic rule of planting design: use the shape and texture of leaves, rather than relying on stronger, brasher flower colour. Unfortunately this runs counter to modern trends, exemplified in many exhibits at flower shows. Chelsea in late May is a riot of blooms, all perfection in themselves, but certainly not restful. A garden or exhibition stand that avoids stridency by using colour in moderation is immediately outstanding. There is no doubt that the simple things in life work best, and this is nowhere more apparent than in the garden.

Key to planting plan

1   *Euonymus fortunei* 'Emerald and Gold'
2   *Cornus stolonifera* 'Flaviramea'
3   *Sambucus racemosa* 'Plumosa Aurea'
4   *Euphorbia epithimoides (polychroma)*
5   *Cytisus scoparius prostratus*
6   *Hosta fortunei* 'Aurea'
7   *Genista sagittalis*
8   *Potentilla arbuscula* 'Gold Finger'
9   *Santolina virens*
10   *Hypericum patulum* 'Hidcote'
11   *Alchemilla mollis*
12   *Gleditsia triacanthos* 'Sunburst'
13   *Elaeagnus pungens* 'Maculata'
14   *Rudbeckia deamii*
15   *Solidago caesia*

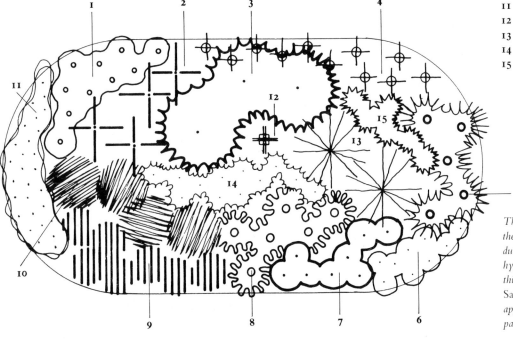

The leaves of Eleagnus pungens *'Maculata' and the stems of* Cornus stolonifera *'Flaviramea' during the winter; the flowers of broom, hypericum and potentilla during summer. Add to this the leaves of* Hosta fortunei *'Aurea' and* Sambucus plumosa *'Aurea' and you will appreciate that good planting design caters for all parts of the year*

INSPIRATION FROM AROUND THE WORLD

It seems remarkable that in a world where cultural differences are rapidly disappearing, gardens still retain national characteristics. It is certainly not due to the local use of plant material, for early exploration and subsequent improvements in communication have ensured that species native to one hemisphere are now commonplace in another. Rhododendron from the Himalayas, phormium and hebe from New Zealand or redwoods from America can be found in many a European park or garden, rubbing shoulders with one another and quite happy to do so.

The greatest influences on garden style are climatic and religious. Although both of these are diminishing in everyday significance, they have set parameters that are still acknowledged. This is largely out of respect for the overriding demands of environment, something that is still difficult to control without enormous capital outlay. It is quite true that gardens can be created in the desert and that the most inhospitable roof garden can be filled with bloom. These are, however, the exceptions: the average person is going to do, in gardening terms, what comes naturally, and this is precisely what gardens are all about.

In Britain a temperate climate allows gardeners an almost free rein over what they can grow. In some ways the rein is altogether too free, a temperate climate gardener is spoilt for choice and the results are often over-complicated. British garden history is long and although not over-distinguished, has produced genius from time to time. There is, I believe, a firm connection between a nation's gardening history and its success in contemporary landscaping terms. The Japanese learnt many of their gardening skills from the Chinese and in both styles the religious overtones are of great importance. It is significant that the Oriental style has spread throughout the world, but as soon as style is divorced from the original spirit of creation, visual success diminishes. In fact, many so-called Japanese gardens are a travesty of the real thing, simply because of lack of understanding.

A sub-tropical climate creates problems of its own. It is certainly a marvellous growing medium, but can be too much of a good thing. Higher temperatures and rainfall make everything grow, not just the chosen subjects! Conditions in a sub-tropical region vary from areas of warmth and moisture, without the hazards of frost, to locations that verge on tropical rain forest. Even within a temperate area, the effects of micro climate or – as in the case of the Scilly Islands – a warm ocean current, can produce a sub-tropical environment.

Travelling abroad and looking at other people's gardens often makes it possible to understand their way of life a little better. If gardeners had more political influence, the world would undoubtedly be a better place!

The stunning pergola at Barnsley House draped with wisteria and under-planted with ornamental onions, all of which leads the eye down the cobbled walk to the delightful focal point at the end

English Gardens

The essence of English gardens is their variety. This is dependent upon the vast range of topography and micro climate in the British Isles. The far north-west coast of Scotland is astonishingly mild, owing to the effects of the Gulf Stream; parts of East Anglia, hundreds of miles further south, regularly record both the lowest and the highest temperatures throughout the year. Courtyards in central London can often be frost-free havens for tender plants, but in the suburbs a few miles away, conditions may be the exact opposite.

To most people 'an English garden' conjures up a soft summer day in the country, meandering paths, herbaceous borders and the background hum of bees. Just such a garden is shown at the bottom of page 159. It has the atmosphere that is unquestionably English. All the elements are there, the mown grass path, roses, lilac and lavender. A gazebo nestles behind the planting, just round the corner. Garden buildings such as this are an intrinsic part of the scene: an old timber summerhouse at the end of a croquet lawn, a rustic garden shelter smothered with the white climbing

The plan of a typically English garden of the type shown at the bottom of page 159. Sweeping borders, a summer house and on the opposite side a shady arbour that looks back across the lawn

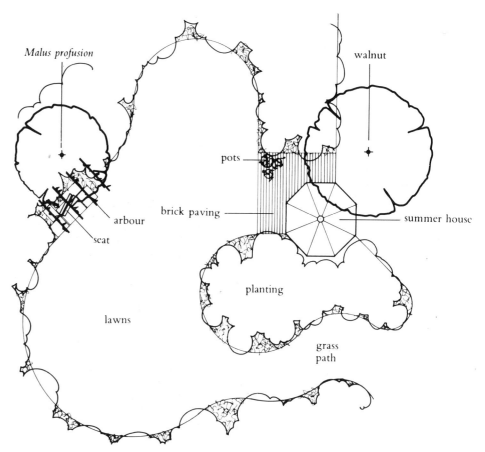

Malus profusion

walnut

pots

brick paving

arbour

seat

summer house

planting

lawns

grass
path

rose 'Swan Lake' or even a delapidated store in a corner of a walled vegetable garden, all have character and all serve a purpose, both visual and practical.

I visit many country gardens, and the common link between them all, however different they may be in concept or style, is their inherent 'rightness' for a given set of circumstances. More often than not they appear unplanned, until it becomes apparent that it is precisely their relaxed atmosphere that makes them work so well.

One of the drawbacks of gardens in this style is that they are intensely personal affairs, usually laid out by a husband and wife team. The problem comes when the garden passes out of their hands; only they know the characteristics of certain plants and only they understand the relationship between, say, a group of trees and the house. Some things, the position of a hedge or pool perhaps, might seem totally irrational to a newcomer, but originally they served a purpose, quite possibly a romantic one – another English garden attribute.

Key to planting plan

1   *Buddleia davidii* 'White Bouquet'
2   *Monarda* 'Cambridge Scarlet'
3   *Lysimachia punctata*
4   *Malva alcea* 'Fastigiata'
5   *Crambe cordifolia*
6   *Euphorbia wulfenii*
7   *Rosa sericea pteracantha*
8   *Rosa* 'Ballerina'
9   *Hebe* 'Midsummer Beauty'
10 *Hibiscus syriacus* 'Woodbridge'
11 *Acanthus spinosa*
12 *Rosa* 'Nevada'
13 *Rosa* 'Max Graf'
14 *Papaver orientalis* 'Black and White'
15 *Euphorbia wallichii*
16 *Geum × borisii*
17 *Geranium* 'Russell Pritchard'
18 *Artemisia* 'Lambrook Silver'
19 *Campanula* 'Ivory Bells'
20 *Anemone japonica* 'Queen Charlotte'
21 *Philadelphus* 'Belle Étoile'
22 *Syringa vulgaris* 'Maud Notcutt'
23 *Rosa* 'Canary Bird'
24 *Aruncus sylvester*
25 *Pulmonaria saccharata* 'Highdown'
26 *Dianthus* 'Doris'
27 *Aster thompsonii* 'Nana'
28 *Dicentra spectabile* 'Alba'
29 climbing rose 'Casino'
30 *Lavandula angustifolia* 'Vera'
31 *Linum narbonnense*
32 *Cytisus × kewensis*
33 *Geranium endressii*
34 *Veronica longifolia* 'Foersters Blue'
35 *Geranium* 'Johnson's Blue'
36 *Sedum spectabile* 'Autumn Joy'
37 *Ruta graveolens* 'Jackman's Blue'
38 *Phlox paniculata* 'Blue Ice'
39 *Rosmarinus officinalis* 'Miss Jessop's Upright'
40 *Hyssopus aristatus*
41 *Geranium sanguineum* 'Album'
42 *Eryngium planum*
43 *Lavatera olbia* 'Rosea'
44 *Polygonum bistorta* 'Superbum'
45 *Rosa willmottiae*
46 *Lavandula angustifolia* 'Vera'
47 *Potentilla* 'Katherine Dykes'
48 *Rosa* 'Madame Butterfly'
49 climbing rose 'Alberic Barbier'

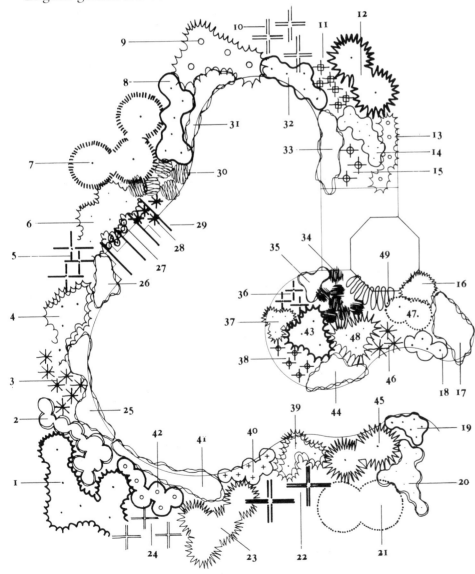

The planting plan for the same garden (page 159). Virtually all of these are softly modelled species that merge with one another to produce an informal and fragrant background. Such a garden, relying on a high proportion of herbaceous material, will look at its best during the summer

On an altogether different plane and scale are the great gardens at Stourhead in Wiltshire. These just predate the major landscape work of Capability Brown and Humphrey Repton. To my mind Stourhead is the better for it, just a little more intimate, if that can be said of a garden that covers hundreds of acres. The photograph below combines the three elements that make Stourhead great, architecture, water and trees. Although the latter two look natural, they are both contrived, just as are the vast number of superb temples that embellish every view with crisp stone colonnades and perfectly proportioned roofs. The house is strangely insignificant in landscape terms, with a half-forgotten ha-ha straddling the

Stourhead is one of England's finest gardens. Set around a lake it contains numerous temples, a grotto and superb mature plantings of trees and shrubs. The use of water to produce perfect reflections is a typically English tradition and increases the feeling of space and tranquility

Another English institution is the pergola and a planting of roses simply reinforces this. An old stone path leads the eye towards the seat where one can sit and contemplate a perfect summers day

A winding grass path almost swamped by planting leads one around to a hidden summerhouse. The combination of surprise and a leisurely route to an objective helps to increase a feeling of space and movement in a garden

parkland on one side. It is a great shame that the ha-ha is such an expensive feature to build. They really are the perfect stock-proof boundary and allow an uninterrupted view of the landscape. This heightens the drama of the woodland walks that surround the lake and climb the encircling slopes. The temples are positioned so that they are 'happened' upon, glimpsed across water or through trees. There is even a grotto, that ultimate decadent landscape feature, with a superb view, back over the lake. Stourhead is built on acid soil and rhododendron has been planted to take full advantage of this. Visit the garden in spring or early summer for a unique and unforgettable experience.

There are two more things in gardening life that are unquestionably English: climbing roses and pergolas. The former have the breath of summer, the latter is totally inert but both are in essence quite inseparable. There are countless roses and as many designs for pergolas: timber, metal or brick, wire frames, trellis arches or a permutation of any of these. In many ways a pergola is the ideal way to grow a climbing plant. If it is against a house or a wall, it may encounter all sorts of problems: lack of light, insufficient water or projecting foundations. A pergola provides an open situation, light, air and access to water in abundance, as well as having that most important attribute, a purpose. Pergolas can frame a view, provide a walkway or divide different parts of the garden.

The pergola at Abbots Ripton Hall in Cambridgeshire, at the top of page 159, does most of these things. For a start, it is host to a wealth of climbing roses, the white tempering, the delicate pink and vibrant red. It is built from simple hoops of iron, mercifully unobtrusive. The trouble with many pergolas is that they are over-complicated, built of great brick piers with weirdly detailed timber cross pieces. Such structures need equally rampant planting if they are not to dominate everything else.

The pathway that leads through the tunnel can, of course, be laid in any material, but I particularly like the combination of staggered York stone and gravel. The latter is always useful groundcover and also acts as a foil for plants growing through the surface. This series of arches also frames a vista, or focal point, as all the best pergolas do. A neatly designed white seat invites anyone who comes to it to sit a while and enjoy the view.

The best pergola occupies the whole of page 154. Laburnum is a striking tree when grown in isolation but even more dramatic when trained, as here, as an avenue over another metal pergola. This particular yellow is often too vibrant when seen against a wider garden setting, but contained as a single element it works very well. The underplanting is strikingly different, being made up of allium, the ornamental onion and that beautiful Welsh poppy, *Meconopsis cambrica*.

A hybrid pergola, again thoroughly British, is the arbour. In this case overhead beams run out from a free-standing wall or house, to form a sitting area. The best arbours not only have climbing plants but soft perennials and shrubs as a margin. Fragrance is the key here: jasmine, honeysuckle, night-scented stocks and nicotiana will create paradise to rival any Persian glorietta (see page 8).

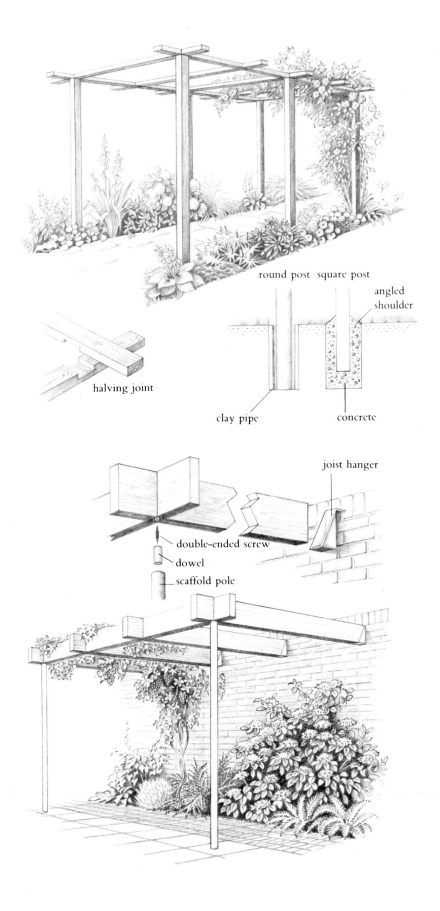

round post square post

angled
shoulder

halving joint

clay pipe

concrete

joist hanger

double-ended screw

dowel

scaffold pole

While pergolas are freestanding structures, overhead beams, or arbours, are usually supported on one side by a wall. The construction of either can follow a multitude of designs, but the best are simple and uncluttered

Japanese Gardens

Above: Raked gravel and boulders – to represent water and land – simple detailing of timbers and minimal planting are all hallmarks of the Japanese style

Above right: A simple foreground and frame of beams helps to emphasise the background of indigenous planting

Opposite: A loose cobble beach, stepping stones, stone lanterns and water combine to produce a strong Japanese influence, although this garden is set in the English countryside. To a purist such a garden seems out of place, but it has considerable charm and certainly offers low maintenance

It seems hard to believe, with the vital role that the Japanese play in the world economy, that until just over 100 years ago little was known of that country. The culture of Japan is both ancient and refined: her garden history goes back at least 1,000 years. Initially Japanese gardens stemmed from Chinese but they very soon developed a strong identity that reflected, on a smaller scale, a varied landscape of mountains, rivers and a rocky, island-strewn coastline. Interwoven with this were strong religious overtones of Zen and Taoism which reinforced the use of a garden for relaxation and meditation. Purists – and I tend to agree with them – feel that a Japanese garden can only be created in Japan and that to make it elsewhere is a mockery. Influence, however, is a different matter and taking an idea or theme that may be woven into the garden pattern of another country is certainly acceptable.

The Japanese awareness of line and simplicity is, perhaps, the most important influence. A Japanese garden may well be full of interest, but it is never 'fussy'. Everything is carefully placed and detailed. Timber decking, bridges and fences are superbly controlled pieces of design. Planting is limited to a careful selection of species that are either placed singly as a focal point, or grouped in drifts to provide background continuity or groundcover. The lessons to be learnt from all this in terms of contemporary Western garden design are enormous and make a travesty of the jumble of unrelated features of which westerners are so often fond.

With simplicity goes colour and here again the Japanese garden is restrained. Azaleas are of course indigenous but such plants are used in controlled groups; the colour of foliage and the shadows set up by rock and trees are far more important. In many gardens only three or four species are used and these might include azalea, bamboo and a single pine.

This is the courtyard of a large office block for which I was asked to create a garden in the Japanese style. Water is used as the central theme, with cobble beaches and timber paths, bridges and decking. A stone lantern was flown in from Japan while planting was kept as simple as possible, a single mature pine being positioned for vertical emphasis

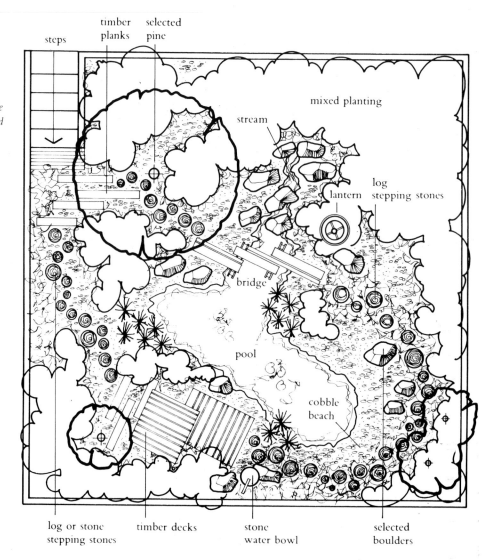

steps

timber planks

selected pine

mixed planting

stream

lantern

log stepping stones

bridge

pool

cobble beach

log or stone stepping stones

timber decks

stone water bowl

selected boulders

Some Japanese features are so attractive that they ask to be reproduced and there is no doubt that the 'Tsukubai' arrangement shown at the bottom of page 165 could form a fascinating feature in a small, enclosed area. Each feature is carefully placed and consists of a protection stone, a front stone and the setting down stone on which the basin (*Tsukubai*) stands. This stone extends to provide room for a water jug or tea kettle. The entire arrangement is a specific part of the traditional tea ceremony and once the philosophy behind it is understood, the feature makes far greater sense and comes alive.

Zen Buddhism exerts the major religious influence on a Japanese garden and a Zen type of garden is usually flat with raked gravel to represent water and boulders to act as islands. The top left illustration on page 162 is a Zen arrangement, the raked gravel indicating a ruffled sea. Where sea and land meet, around the boulders, waves and ripples are set up in exactly the same way as they would be in a natural environment. The lower, more distant island has a carefully positioned plant, indicating a tree or even a forest in the larger landscape.

The picture on the opposite page is rather different, however, reproducing a mood rather than a specific Japanese style. The ingredients are there, certainly: loose cobbles running in a beach down to the water, rocks and a carefully positioned lantern. Azaleas and a stunningly autumnal maple add to the picture, but as yet look a little too young to be really effective. The use of random stepping stones through the cobble 'sea' is also a traditional ingredient and an attractive one, that can be readily translated into a Western garden in a variety of forms, including man-made slabs and timber.

Gates and entrances are an important feature in Japanese gardens, there normally being a main gate for family and visitors, and a rear 'sweeping gate' for the removal of rubbish. Moon gates were essentially Chinese, although the Japanese also used pierced screens and walls to embrace a view of the landscape where this was permissible. The idea of linking house with garden and finally with the landscape beyond is eminently sensible and works well in any country. All too often people surround themselves with an impenetrable boundary, simply through lack of thought and a leaning towards convention. Very often the inclusion of a view, or at least the sight of trees and foliage from an adjoining plot, can enhance a garden enormously.

A gardener in the position shown at the top right of page 162 would be mad not to draw the surrounding area into the composition. In effect, this is a Japanese interpretation, a controlled foreground with rock and raked gravel framed by the austere walkway, roof and timber uprights. The tracery of trees is excellent and in a situation such as this, lower branches can be trimmed and removed, to enhance the view and improve the sculptural line of the trunks.

Moss provides the ideal floor in a low-use situation, moulding itself to contours and acting as a unifying element to the foliage above. The maples once again make a striking contribution.

Japanese arrrangement of stone bowl, water flume, boulders and planting. Such a feature could be used in many situations and the sound of water falling into the bowl is delightful

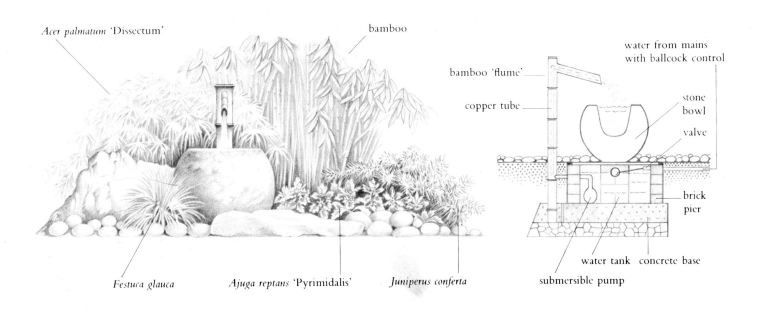

Acer palmatum 'Dissectum'

bamboo

Festuca glauca

Ajuga reptans 'Pyrimidalis'

Juniperus conferta

water from mains with ballcock control

bamboo 'flume'

copper tube

stone bowl

valve

brick pier

water tank   concrete base

submersible pump

Chinese Gardens

I have already said that religion and symbolism have probably provided the strongest influence on garden design, certainly during its formative period, in whatever country it arose. Thousands of years ago, empires held sway over vast tracts of land but communications were so poor and physical obstacles so immense that contact between cultures was virtually non-existent. In any case, links between adjoining empires were more often than not discouraged, secrets were jealously guarded and what information did leak along the myriad of trade routes was usually distorted or deliberately untrue.

While Rome was extending her influence throughout the Middle East and Europe, the Emperors of China controlled territories that reached from Korea to the depths of Asia. It was their contact with Korea that enabled the Japanese later to develop their own garden style (see previous chapter).

By the time Christ was born, there is documented evidence that Chinese garden design, under the Han Dynasty, was flourishing. The gardens were enormous and included parks for hunting, colossal water gardens and complex systems of hills and valleys. At first they were solely the preserve of the ruling class, but as time went on, they became commonplace among the rich and even the not so well off on a far more intimate scale. Although Roman gardens contained house gods, they were not primarily places for worship, but designed rather more for relaxation and recreation. In China meditation was far more important and the garden became very much a part of Taoist nature worship.

In many ways the development of the Chinese gardens was similar to

Although this is a Chinese garden it relates to modern courtyards in the West. The invitation into an outdoor room is there, the delicate floor allows use at all times and the walls provide shelter. The rocks are pure sculpture while the delicate branches introduce an essential natural ingredient

that of the English landscape school: both were idealized and both reflected contemporary styles in painting. The later Chinese gardens became rather more intimate: the parks dwindled to walled areas, water was used in all its guises, grottos were popular and so, too, were garden buildings, carefully-positioned trees and shrubs.

The use of rock, so characterised in the Japanese style, is directly borrowed from China where enormous pieces were set with great care to represent a hill or mountain.

One of the most important elements within a garden is the use of open and closed views. This was particularly apparent in country gardens, where a sweeping landscape could be contrasted with a crisply detailed courtyard, but although views were less obvious in urban areas, the same approach was still valid.

The small picture on the right illustrates this treatment precisely. To the left the view fans out to the distant pavillions with their precisely designed architectural roofs. Immediately ahead lies a delicate but simple octagonal window, framing the view of tree stems, foliage and carefullly sited rock. It is, in fact, this contrast between an inherently plain but effective foreground and the more complex and intimate background that brings the composition to life. The one emphasises the other. Chinese design often takes the form of juxtaposition of the complex and the simple, of shadow and sunlight. Here, the geometric fence becomes even more telling when seen against plain walls and slender timber uprights.

Open and closed views are a vital part of the Chinese garden tradition. So too is the juxtaposition of plain floors and walls with the more intimate nature of planting. Both these photographs show windows where a glimpse into an area can be gained. Notice too how shadow is intentionally cast onto the simple wall in the upper illustration, to provide a contrast in light and shade

Translated into Western terms, this approach has much to teach. Each element of the design takes on a specific purpose, which is not only an entity in itself, but also relates to the surrounding garden and more distant landscape. If this philosophy were practised in the West, there would be a deal less clutter and a lot more sense.

The strange yet dramatic waterworn rocks on page 166 are also set within the boundaries of a walled courtyard. Here the main view is outward from the house, the open shutters emphasizing the way into the garden. The delicate wooden tracery works in contrast to the crisp vertical frames and is echoed by the equally delicate shapes of branches silhouetted against the white background.

The floor is interesting, a chequer board of black and white stones. These are tiny cobbles set in courses within the individual squares, another example of the extreme care and thought that goes into every square inch of the overall composition. In many ways the floor is reminiscent of the tiled floors so popular with the Victorians and reflects a surprising similarity in thought, for both societies were preoccupied with the minutiae of design.

At the very beginning of this book, in the section on conservatories, there are French windows framing a view into the garden. That garden and the Chinese example are thousands of miles apart, but in essence their design does much the same thing: it focuses on a composition and invites one outside to enjoy it.

The final illustration, at the top of page 167, shows the extreme delicacy of a well-handled small space. There is an overriding architectural line here that uses walls, windows and timber screen work to surround a carefully pruned small tree.

All the 'bright light' countries need the contrast of light and shadow to emphasize certain aspects of a garden design. The great Italian Renaissance compositions and the Moorish Courts are particularly good examples of this, but both of them used the transition between light and shade in a basic manner, whether it was the shadow cast by a line of cypress on a Mediterranean hillside or the transition between a cool interior and the glaring white walls of the Alhambra in Spain. The Chinese took the art a great deal further, using a tree or bush and pruning it carefully to cast a delicate tracery on to a background surface. There is a direct visual relationship between the man-made wooden screens and the natural shadow, emphasising the similarity between the two while at the same time underlining the importance of nature within a pattern, however contrived.

These ideas in the context of contemporary gardening are refreshing and instructive. There is a similarity between timber screens and a modern concrete screen block wall. The Chinese understood the need to set a complicated pattern within an understated background, to balance hard and soft, and light and shade so creating a pleasing harmony overall. It is this perfect balance attained by intuition that is so often missing from our western designs.

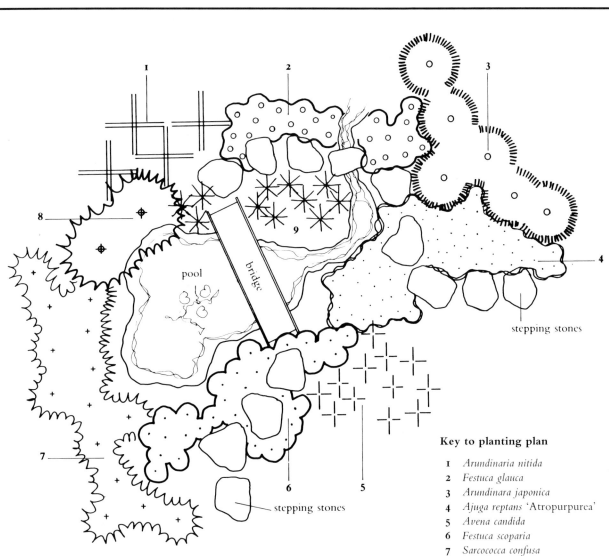

pool

bridge

stepping stones

stepping stones

Key to planting plan

1 *Arundinaria nitida*
2 *Festuca glauca*
3 *Arundinara japonica*
4 *Ajuga reptans* 'Atropurpurea'
5 *Avena candida*
6 *Festuca scoparia*
7 *Sarcococca confusa*
8 *Acer japonicum* 'Aureum'
9 *Molinia caerulea* 'Variegata'

A garden in the Japanese style surrounding a pool and small stream. The planting is built up from taller growing bamboos and lower ground hugging grasses combined with true groundcovers such as ajuga and sarcococca

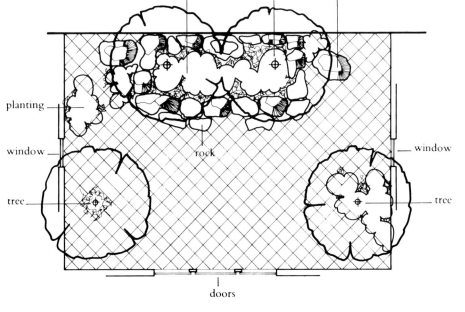

planting   trees   standing stones

planting

window

tree

window

tree

rock

doors

Plan of the illustration on page 166. It clearly shows the simplicity of the design and also the formality, one side being virtually a mirror image of the other

Sub-tropical Gardens

To those who live in temperate or even colder regions, there is a certain romance about the word sub-tropical. It calls up visions of a Mediterranean landscape with sun-drenched villas and yards of bouganvillia twining their way over pergolas and terracotta pantiles. However, a sub-tropical climate can range from the near temperate to almost tropical conditions. The range of habitat is enormous. The direct benefits of a warm ocean current such as the Gulf Stream, are plain to see in the Scilly Islands, south-west of the tip of Cornwall. Here, in the famous gardens of Tresco Abbey, created by Augustus Smith over a century ago, are species found nowhere else in Europe, including ironwoods from New Zealand and Mexican yuccas. So mild are the

An undeniably Mediterranean garden with its old brick floor and massive arbour supports, terra cotta pots against an old plaster wall, and ample trees to cast shade and temper the inevitable bright light

Left and above: *Tresco Abbey, set in the Scilly Isles, off Cornwall is a haven for many sub-tropical plants. Warmed by the Gulf Stream and virtually frost free it offers a home for a vast range of species*

conditions that several species have colonized areas outside the gardens, agapanthus and tree lupins being two examples.

One disadvantage of an island environment is the predominance of a salt laden atmosphere and planting has to be either tolerant of these conditions or given shelter by trees and walling. In fact many of the most spectacular Tresco plants are to be seen growing at the base, or on the face, of superb stone walls, as seen in the larger picture above, which shows a variety of succulents often found only as house plants on the mainland. Such a wall provides a deep, cool root run that drains freely, ideal for such species. On an aesthetic level the colour range is excellent: reds, yellows and oranges combining to form a composition all within one range and green foliage creating a restful background. The wall itself is superbly constructed and laid 'dry' with large pieces of granite. This allows easy colonization by plants and eliminates the dreadful suburban tendency to use toothpaste-like mortar, squeezing out from between the joints. Like all the best walls this one is constructed with a slight 'batter', meaning that the base is wider than the top. This helps light and air to reach all the plants more easily. On a far larger scale, the monkey puzzle trees form an

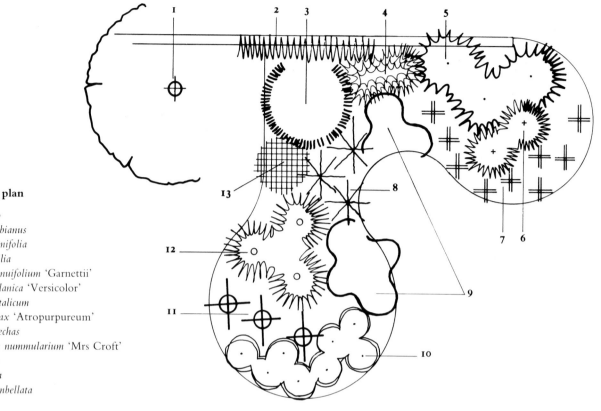

Key to planting plan

1   *Arbutus unedo*
2   *Ceanothus lobbianus*
3   *Baccharis halimifolia*
4   *Cantua buxifolia*
5   *Pittosporum tenuifolium 'Garnettii'*
6   *Fuchsia magellanica 'Versicolor'*
7   *Helichrysum italicum*
8   *Phormium tenax 'Atropurpureum'*
9   *Lavandula stoechas*
10 *Helianthemum nummularium 'Mrs Croft'*
11 *Salvia fulgens*
12 *Hebe hulkeana*
13 *Raphiolepis umbellata*

This planting plan uses tender material that needs a frost free environment throughout the year. In such a situation, however, plants flourish and grow at a pace that seems impossible in harsher climates

effective background; they have an architectural line that can be particularly effective in the right setting. A small front garden is not one of them!

The photograph on page 170 shows a Mediterranean garden, situated in the warmth of the South of France. It has all the classic ingredients of a gloriously lazy outdoor room. Best of all perhaps from a designer's point of view, it seems uncontrived and this is the highest accolade for any composition. It also has a pleasing degree of austerity, in keeping with an inherently dry climate. The massive tapering pergola supports are in direct contrast to the simply fashioned overhead beams but are reinforced by the towering golden conifer in the background. The trees act as a soft foil to the severe lines of walling and paving. The latter have been loosly bedded on the soil below so that they follow the contours of the ground, reinforcing the informality of the design. The terracotta pots are casual and so, too, is the furniture. This is a comfortable place for eating, drinking or simply relaxing.

Colour is kept to a minimum, the blue at the base of the column being compatible with the pink blossom. It underlines the point that less often means far more in terms of design. Too much colour here would have ruined the effect. As to the effect of light on a composition, the stronger it is – and its strength increases with the height of the sun – the more pallid colour becomes. This is precisely why strong hues work well in a sub-tropical, bright, light country. They are in effect watered down. Bedding displays of tropical species, out of context, produce a garish result. Native

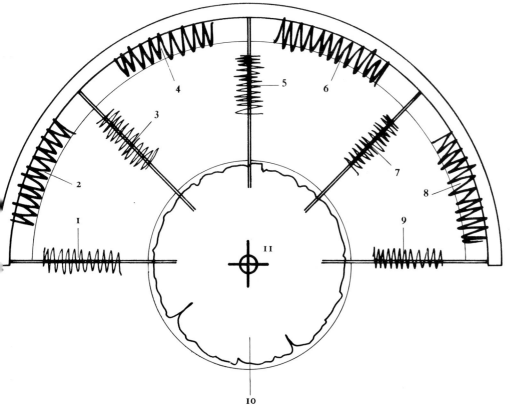

Key to planting plan

1 *Juniperus angulare*
2 *Holboellia latifolia*
3 *Pandorea jasminoides*
4 *Clematis hookerana*
5 *Campsis radicans*
6 *Clematis napaulensis*
7 *Lonicera splendida*
8 *Passiflora antioquiensis*
9 *Solanum jasminoides*
10 *Lavandula stoechas*
11 *Cordyline australis*

An unusual curved wall and pergola that pivots around a central bed of French lavender and a single cordyline. The climbers are all varieties that would thrive in a Mediterranean climate forming a delightful canopy

British wild flowers do not, in the main, have harsh contours; most of them are moderate, like the climate and light values!

The final illustration in this section, at the top right of page 171, is also of Tresco Abbey. Here at last is that glorious Mediterranean plant, bouganvillia, a twisting, rampant scrambler that can cover a tree, wall or building in a mass of dark pink flowers. In terms of planting design, this is another success and the contrasting foliage shapes throw one another into sharp relief. Another thing that seperates these species from those growing in colder latitudes is the scale of leaf and plant. Large leaves offer enormous areas for photosynthesis and consequent rapid growth. They are, as a result, extremely susceptible to temperature changes and frost-free conditions are therefore essential. Notice how the pale blue sky and the massive leaves to one side, tone down the vibrant bouganvillia.

In many ways a sub-tropical garden is more dependent on rainfall than on anything else. The Scilly Isles have approximately 82 cm (32 in) of rain per year: much less than that and the range of species is severely limited, much more and the climate is verging on tropical conditions, with a huge increase in the range of plants available.

Britain can thank those great Victorian plant collectors, not just for summer bedding but for nearly all the house and conservatory species. It is appropriate that Tresco, which is probably the finest sub-tropical garden in Europe, was a Victorian creation. It reflects the foresight of a generation that had not only the time but the means to collect and bring home unique plants that have changed the face of gardening.

GARDEN FEATURES

This book has looked at gardens of every description, large, small, woodland and water. The common denominator is excellence. Nearly all the compositions have had a theme and these have been considered in great detail, to discover how a particular style or personality has fashioned a garden in a unique manner. No two designs are ever alike, not because of differences in site, situation or soil, but because of the whims and tastes of the owner.

It may well be that gardens are becoming ever smaller and that the pressures on them are ever more demanding but I firmly believe that they are also becoming more personal. Because of limitations of size, much of their individuality is due to the choice of furnishings and features.

Many of the gardens I design are for the planning service of a well-known periodical. Virtually all the sites are less than a quarter of an acre and a special section in the questionnaire covers the features needed. These can range from pots, pools and lighting to birdbaths, dovecots or parterre vegetable gardens. There is simply no accounting for taste – and I mean this in a perfectly polite way.

One of the things I have tried to do throughout this book is to show how things relate to one another in a compatible manner. A bed edged

Below and opposite: Garden features are the furnishings of gardens, they breathe life into a composition and are consequently intensely personal items. Pots are of course essential in virtually any position and I particularly like the column shown below which sets up an interesting relationship with the clipped box to its left

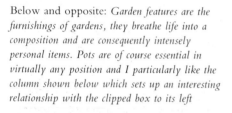

with shells may look appalling in the city but fine outside a seaside guest house. An irregular pond looks terrible in a crisply detailed terrace but acceptable in the more distant reaches of a garden. It is all a matter of commonsense.

One of the major difficulties is choice. Gardening is a growth industry, one of the few, and as such there is a proliferation of garden centres and nurseries selling every conceivable gadget and feature. Resist the temptation to impulse buy; it may be fun at the time but it inevitably results in a dog's dinner later!

The real criterion of whether a feature 'works' is its prominence in the overall garden pattern. With a very few exceptions, a feature should create interest without being overpowering, whether it is a seat acting as a focal point, a sundial at the end of a pergola, or the pergola itself. Under the general classification of feature also comes furnishings: in fact, in many ways, the two are inseperable.

Of course there is a situation where a feature is built up from individual components. We have already seen how a conifer garden or bed can be a striking focal point, yet it is the amalgamation of different plants that produce the overall character. A herb garden is another example, the outline of hedges or low brick walls acting as a framework to the foliage within. Both of these features are fluid, the planting being subject to change, but the overall pattern remains the same.

In a domestic situation, pots and containers certainly come under this heading, as the picture on page 174 shows. Pots are the most manageable way to make plants mobile and are indispensible for bringing instant colour and interest to an otherwise lifeless or bare place. In a new garden, and particularly on a large terrace or patio, pots create a sense of life right away. Sometimes the pot or container provides interest in itself: at home I

Pots come in all shapes and sizes, terra cotta, timber Versailles tubs and glazed earthenware. In general terms the bigger the container the better, allowing a liberal root run

always have one or two empty ones, their shape and material acting as a foil for those around them.

The pot may also become incidental, as most have done in the photograph on page 175, taken at Barnsley House; the plants spread out and conceal the edges. I have a collection of old buckets, chamber pots and boilers, all of which are totally disguised by foliage. In another much-prized chamber pot with a glorious flowered print I plant a delicate pelargonium, and the combination is charming.

It is, of course, the depth and size of pot that is all important. Steer clear of containers that are shallow or too cramped, for these dry out rapidly and there is nothing more heartbreaking than returning after a holiday to find parched or dead plants.

Look out for the unusual. I once planted a superb herb garden in an old bath tub that provided the ideal growing conditions, deep enough for a layer of broken crocks at the bottom and with a ready-made drain hole. It looked what it was, a lot of fun and a real feature in the corner of a tiny basement garden where access to the soil was almost impossible.

I have also seen plants in an old lavatory, but in this case irrigation was by means of a modified cistern, which is really taking things too far!

Herb collections are ideal in pots, as the container limits the more rampant varieties. There are some herbs in the pots at Barnsley, including mint, fennel and sage. The real eye-catcher is the variegated ivy that will provide interest throughout the year. In many ways, this grouping of pots softens the junction between house and terrace perfectly: it is hard to tell where one starts and the other ends.

A feature can be taken out of context and the delightful plinth in the smaller picture on page 174 was no doubt destined for a sober piece of Victoriana. It has a great deal of intrinsic interest and I particularly like the spiral pattern with its strong vertical emphasis. It forms that classic

Garden geometry can often be boring, but this little gem would provide interest even when the planting fades

triangular pattern that works so well everywhere, in Japanese design and here in an English cottage garden. The column forms the high line, the clipped box the middle ground, while a drift of dead nettle carpets the floor at the lowest level. Remove any one of the components and the composition fails; together they cannot be faulted. One of the unexpected pleasures of a strange garden is coming upon such things purely by chance, which makes them all the more effective. This is also a very safe combination and underlines the point I made much earlier about there being specific rules of garden design. This is one of the rules, and it rarely fails.

The point about pots and planting reviving an intrinsically dull background is reinforced by the second picture on the same page. Here terracotta creates a definite theme against the simple precast concrete flags, preferable to some busier paving material. The planted containers form the lower and middle ground against the higher foliage and in particular the soaring hollyhocks. Much of the background is sensibly undemonstrative, the foreground planting providing instant colour. The other point about terracotta is that it is not only a good landscape colour but relates to architecture and brick particularly well. Clay pots are particularly suitable for planting.

Where the last paving pattern was undemonstrative, the one in the corner of the garden at York Gate above left is the exact opposite, rather too busy, but certainly both effective and unusual. This is the central point of a walkway and the eye is led down one side to focus on a planted bowl at the end. The basic pattern of triangles is built up from solid granite setts, infilled with loose gravel. The stone, although complicated, provides a visual link with the house in the background, the old clipped yew trees adding to the air of maturity.

Flanking the path are beds or iris and such a bold planting scheme does

English vegetable gardens so often lack imagination but this one at Barnsley House is a beauty with brick paths dividing the various crops. The seat set under a trellis arbour seems just right for a tired gardener

much to complement the stone walkway. When the flowers fade, however, the picture is likely to be rather drab and sombre. This is of course one problem about recording a scene photographically: it catches a moment and fails to take into account the rest of the year. However, for anyone prepared to wait for a bold and spectacular splash of colour, this will work very well. It also presupposes a garden of ample size in which to indulge such whims. I find it all a bit surreal, particularly the empty wicker baskets on their black plinths.

Barnsley House has a garden of great character, not least of which is the vegetable knot garden (shown left) in which brick paths separate the beds and provide access.

Most vegetable gardens, at least in Britain, are inconceivably boring, as any train journey proves. The trouble with the British is that they are over-zealous: they adore dismal gardening programmes and toil endlessly to produce the perfect Savoy cabbage or King Edward potato! The French, in direct contrast, take things less seriously and I thoroughly applaud their techniques of putting vegetables in the flower border. After all many vegetables are goodlooking, so why keep them hidden from view in some far-flung allotment?

However, a well laid out vegetable garden is superb and should be brought close to the house where it can fulfil a decorative as well as a functional role.

At Barnsley the intention was to create a set piece and it works very well indeed. In many ways it looks back to the parterres considered earlier. It uses a regular geometric pattern and the thing I like best of all is the little

Garden lighting can transform almost any design and extends the length of time one can sit outside. From indoors the results are equally important but remember that simplicity is the key to success

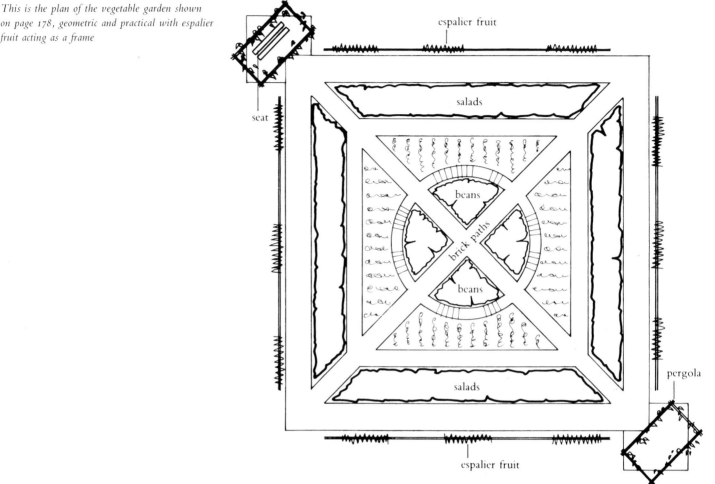

This is the plan of the vegetable garden shown on page 178, geometric and practical with espalier fruit acting as a frame

arbour and seat, where the weary gardener can rest and contemplate his hard work. The best plants for such a place might be a sweet-smelling honeysuckle or rose, or the more utilitarian but spectacular runner bean, a marvellous climber in its own right.

Winter brings a dormant season and a period of inactivity for the gardener, and early nightfall limits the use of the garden even more. Until comparatively recently there was little to be done about this but the advent of garden lighting has not only extended use of the outside room but introduced a new visual dimension.

Lighting basically falls into two broad categories: utilitarian and decorative. The former takes care of paths, garages, drives and the patio or terrace areas that immediately adjoin the house. The style of light fittings has improved enormously in recent years. Gone are the garish and ugly spotlights, replaced by well-designed delicate fittings that can be ground – or wall – mounted. The basic rule, as always, is simplicity: it is the light and not the fitting that should be obvious.

The illustration on page 179 shows this particularly well: apart from the table light all other sources of illumination are concealed. It is dusk, the magic time when garden lighting makes a bridge between night and day.

Pool lighting came into the section on water gardens when I stressed the

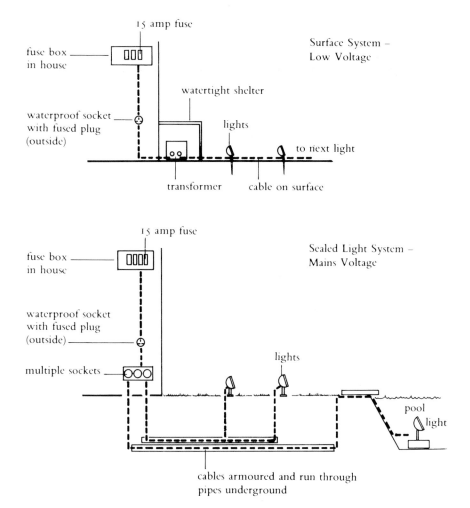

15 amp fuse

fuse box
in house

Surface System –
Low Voltage

watertight shelter

waterproof socket
with fused plug
(outside)

lights

to next light

transformer   cable on surface

15 amp fuse

fuse box
in house

Sealed Light System –
Mains Voltage

waterproof socket
with fused plug
(outside)

lights

multiple sockets

pool
light

cables armoured and run through
pipes underground

Correct installation is essential if you are going to use electricity in the garden. If in doubt consult a specialist, it could be worth it

importance of avoiding the holographic display. The pool here is mercifully simple, an underwater spot just highlighting the bubble fountain that disturbs the surface of the water.

The overhead beams, smothered in climbers, frame the picture; the monstera to the left has been brought outside for the warm summer months. House plants benefit from a breath of fresh air and should be taken into the garden more often.

White furniture is effective during the day, but even more telling in the evening in a softly lighted garden. A meal or drinks take on an altogether more romantic air, and it is possible to imagine for a few short summer months that this is indeed a sub-tropical, Mediterranean garden.

This book is all about creativity. As a designer I see more of it than most people, although it is not common and frequently comes about quite unexpectedly. It is more often than not a simple solution to a complex problem, although some of the great gardens are most certainly creative in both concept and construction.

A final glimpse of creativity is the picture on page 183. An English garden in early summer, with roses and paeonies divided by old stone walls. A green lawn and broad steps invite you to the next garden room from which you will see yet another view that must be full of promise.

PLANT LISTS

KEY

cvs – cultivars ssp – species ✱ – evergreen C – climber S – spreading U – upright I – invasive D – dense shade O – open situation

	COMMON NAME	HEIGHT	HABIT	COMMENTS
TREES AND SHRUBS FOR SHELTER BELTS AND SCREENS				
✱*Arundinaria*	Bamboo	3 to 4.5 m (10 to 15 ft)	S	
Betula	Birch	3.6 to 15 m (12 to 50 ft)	U	attractive bark
✱*Berberis × stenophylla*	Barberry	2.1 to 2.7 m (7 to 9 ft)	S	yellow flowers in spring
✱*Cedrus deodara*	Deodar	15 to 27 m (50 to 90 ft)	S	
✱*Cotoneaster* 'Cornubia'		4.5 to 7.6 m (15 to 25 ft)	S	red berries
✱*Cryptomeria japonica* 'Elegans'	Japanese Cedar	7.6 to 12 m (25 to 40 ft)	S	
✱*Cupressocyparis leylandii*	Leyland Cypress	15 to 27 m (50 to 90 ft)	S	extremely fast grower
✱*Cupressus macrocarpa* 'Lutea'	Golden Monterey Cypress	7.6 to 12 m (25 to 40 ft)	S	
✱*Elaeagnus × ebbingei*		1.5 to 2.1 m (5 to 7 ft)	S	suitable for seaside
✱*Escallonia* cvs		1.2 to 3 m (4 to 10 ft)	S	pink, red or white flowers; suitable for seaside
✱*Eucalyptus*	Gum	12 to 27 m (40 to 90 ft)	U	attractive bark
✱*Ligustrum*	Privet	2.1 to 3.3 m (7 to 11 ft)	S	
✱*Pinus nigra*	Austrian Pine	12 to 21.3 m (40 to 70 ft)	S	suitable for seaside
Populus nigra 'Italica'	Lombardy Poplar	18 to 27 m (60 to 90 ft)	U	
Polygonum baldschuanicum	Russian Vine	4.5 to 9 m (15 to 30 ft)	C	vigorous; white flowers
Prunus avium	Green, Wild Cherry	7.6 to 13.7 m (25 to 45 ft)	S	white flowers
Prunus cerasifera 'Pissardii'	Purple Leaved Plum	4.5 to 7.6 m (15 to 25 ft)	S	young foliage dark red turning purple
✱*Prunus laurocerasus*	Common Laurel, Cherry Laurel	3 to 5.4 m (10 to 18 ft)	S	
✱*Pyracantha*	Firethorn	2.7 to 4.8 m (9 to 16 ft)	S	white flowers; orange berries; thorns
✱*Rhododendron ponticum*		4.5 to 7.6 m (15 to 25 ft)	S	purple flowers in spring
Rosa 'Fruhlingsgold'		1.8 to 3.6 m (6 to 12 ft)	S	fragrant pale yellow single flowers
Sorbus aria 'Lutescens'	Whitebeam	6 to 12 m (20 to 40 ft)	U	white felt on undersides of leaves
✱*Thuya plicata*	Western Red Cedar	7.6 to 13.7 m (25 to 45 ft)	S	
TREES AND SHRUBS FOR SANDY SOIL				
Amelanchier canadensis	Snowy Mespilus	3.6 to 5.4 m (12 to 18 ft)	S	white flowers; autumn colour
Atriplex halimus	Tree Purslane	1.5 to 1.8 m (5 to 6 ft)	S	silver foliage; suitable for seaside
Buddleia cvs	Butterfly Bush	1.8 to 3 m (6 to 10 ft)	S	flowers attract butterflies
Caryopteris × clandonensis	Blue Spiraea	45 to 75 cm (1½ to 2½ ft)	S	late blue flowers; tolerates lime
✱*Cistus*	Sun Rose	45 cm to 1.8 m (1½ to 6 ft)	S	flowers pink or white; suitable for seaside; tolerates lime
✱*Convolvulus cneorum*		45 to 60 cm (1½ to 2 ft)	S	silver foliage; white flowers
Cytisus cvs	Broom	45 cm to 1.8 m (1½ to 6 ft)	S	flowers white, or shades of yellow and red; tolerates lime
✱*Daboecia cantabrica*	St Daboec's Heath	23 to 30 cm (9 to 12 in)	S	pink flowers; lime-free soil
✱*Embothrium coccineum*	Chilean Fire Bush	3 to 4.2 m (10 to 14 ft)	U	orange flowers; semi evergreen; lime-free soil
✱*Erica* cvs	Heath	15 cm to 2.4 m (6 in to 8 ft)	S	colour and form varies
Erinacea anthyllis	Hedgehog Broom	23 to 30 cm (9 to 12 in)	S	blue flowers; spines
✱*Escallonia* cvs		1.2 to 3 m (4 to 10 ft)	S	pink, red or white flowers; suitable for seaside
✱*Euonymus* cvs		45 cm to 2.4 m (1½ to 8 ft)	S	
Genista	Broom	60 cm to 3 m (2 to 10 ft)	S	yellow flowers
✱*Hebe* cvs	Shrubby Veronica	15 cm to 1.2 m (6 in to 4 ft)	S	white or lilac flowers; suitable for seaside
✱*Lavandula* cvs	Lavender	45 cm to 1 m (1½ to 3 ft)	S	aromatic grey foliage; pink or mauve flowers
✱*Lupinus arboreus*	Tree Lupin	1.2 to 2.1 (4 to 7 ft)	S	yellow flowers
Lycium	Box Thorn	1.5 to 2.1 m (5 to 7 ft)	S	scrambler with violet flowers and berries
✱*Olearia*	Daisy Bush	1 to 1.5 m (3 to 5 ft)	S	white flowers; suitable for seaside
Philadelphus cvs	Mock Orange	1.8 to 4.5 m (6 to 15 ft)	S	fragrant white flowers
✱*Pieris*	Lily-of-the-valley Tree	1.8 to 6 m (6 to 20 ft)	S	several cvs have young red foliage
Potentilla fruticosa	Shrubby Cinquefoil	30 cm to 1.5 m (1 to 5 ft)	S	yellow flowers
Romneya coulteri	Tree Poppy	1.2 to 1.8 m (4 to 6 ft)	S	large white fragrant flowers
✱*Rosmarinus*	Rosemary	15 cm to 1.8 m (6 in to 6 ft)	S/U	aromatic foliage
✱*Santolina incana (chamaecyparissus)*	Cotton Lavender	38 cm to 1 m (15 in to 3 ft)	S	silver foliage
✱*Senecio* 'Sunshine'		1 to 1.5 m (3 to 5 ft)	S	grey foliage; yellow flowers; suitable for seaside
Spartium junceum	Spanish Broom	1.8 to 2.4 m (6 to 8 ft)	S	yellow flowers; suitable for seaside
✱*Tamarix tetrandra*	Tamarisk	2.4 to 3.5 m (8 to 12 ft)	S	pink flowers; suitable for seaside
Ulex	Gorse	1.2 to 2.4 m (4 to 8 ft)	S	yellow flowers; suitable for seaside
Vaccinium corymbosum	American Blueberry	1.5 to 1.8 m (5 to 6 ft)	S	edible blue berries; lime-free soil
✱*Yucca*		1.2 to 3 m (6 to 10 ft)	U	tall cream flower spike; suitable for seaside

	COMMON NAME	HEIGHT	HABIT	COMMENTS

TREES AND SHRUBS FOR CHALKY SOIL

	COMMON NAME	HEIGHT	HABIT	COMMENTS
Aralia chinensis	Chinese Angelica Tree	3 to 4.5 m (10 to 15 ft)	S	huge clusters of white flowers
★*Aucuba japonica* cvs	Spotted Laurel	1.5 to 2.7 m (5 to 9 ft)	S	
★*Berberis × lologensis*	Barberry	2.1 to 2.7 m (7 to 9 ft)	S	yellow flowers
Betula	Birch	4.5 to 12 m (15 to 40 ft)	S/U	decorative bark
Buddleia cvs	Butterfly Bush	1.8 to 3 m (6 to 10 ft)	S	flowers attract butterflies
★*Bupleurum fruticosum*		1.5 to 3 m (5 to 10 ft)	S	yellow flowers; suitable for seaside
★*Buxus*	Box	1 to 2.4 m (3 to 8 ft)	S	
★*Carpenteria californica*		1.8 to 2.4 m (5 to 8 ft)	S	large white flowers
Carpinus	Hornbeam	7.6 to 18 m (25 to 60 ft)	S/U	good for hedging
Celastrus orbiculatus		7.6 to 9 m (25 to 30 ft)	C	twiner; attractive fruits
Chaenomeles speciosa cvs	Flowering Quince	2.1 to 4.5 m (7 to 15 ft)	S	early flowers in shades of pink, red and white
★*Choisya ternata*	Mexican Orange Blossom	2.4 to 3.6 m (8 to 12 ft)	S	fragrant white flowers
★*Cistus*	Rock Rose	15 cm to 1.8 m (6 in to 6 ft)	S	pink or white flowers; suitable for seaside
Clematis cvs		3 to 9 m (10 to 30 ft)	C	flowers vary in form and colour
Clerodendron trichotonum		3 to 3.6 m (10 to 12 ft)	S	white fragrant flowers; blue berries
Cornus	Dogwood	1.8 to 6 m (6 to 20 ft)	S	some kinds have coloured stems
★*Corokia cotoneaster*	Wire-netting bush	1.8 to 2.4 m (6 to 8 ft)	S	small yellow flowers; orange fruits
Cotoneaster horizontalis		30 to 38 cm (12 to 15 in)	S	red berries; good wall shrub
Crataegus	Thorn	4.5 to 7.6 m (15 to 25 ft)	S	haws; autumn colour
Cytisus cvs		45 cm to 1.8 m (1½ to 6 ft)	S	flowers white, or shades of red or yellow
Deutzia cvs		1.2 to 2.1 m (4 to 7 ft)	S	pink or white flowers
Dipelta		1.8 to 4.5 m (6 to 15 ft)	S	pink or cream flowers
★*Elaeagnus*		1.8 to 2.7 m (6 to 9 ft)	S	suitable for seaside
★*Erica herbacea* cvs	Heather	15 to 38 cm (6 to 9 in)	S	winter flowering
Erica terminalis	Corsican Heath	1 to 1.8 m (3 to 6 ft)	U	pink flowers
Erinacea anthyllis	Hedgehog Broom	23 to 30 cm (9 to 12 in)	S	blue flowers; spines
★*Escallonia* cvs		1.2 to 3 m (4 to 10 ft)	S	pink, red or white flowers; suitable for seaside
★*Euonymus*		45 cm to 2.4 m (1½ to 8 ft)	S	choose evergreen varieties with variegated foliage
Fagus sylvatica	Beech	18 to 24 m (60 to 80 ft)	S	good for hedging
Forsythia		2.7 to 4.5 m (9 to 15 ft)	U	yellow flowers
Fuchsia cvs		1 to 2.1 m (3 to 7 ft)	S	flower colour varies with cv
Genista hispanica	Spanish Gorse	60 cm to 3 m (2 to 10 ft)	S	yellow flowers
★*Hebe*	Shrubby Speedwell	15 cm to 1.2 m (6 in to 4 ft)	S	white or lilac flowers; suitable for seaside
★*Hedera* cvs	Ivy	4.5 to 12 m (15 to 40 ft)	C	many cvs have variegated foliage
Hibiscus cvs	Rose Mallow	2.1 to 4.2 m (7 to 14 ft)	U	late flowers in shades of pink, violet and white
★*Hypericum calycinum*	Rose of Sharon	15 to 23 cm (6 to 9 in)	S	vigorous; large yellow flowers
Jasminum	Jasmine	2.4 to 4.2 m (8 to 14 ft)	S	winter and summer flowering kinds
Kerria japonica 'Pleniflora'	Jew's Mallow	1.5 to 2.4 m (5 to 8 ft)	S	yellow flowers; green stems
Kolkwitzia amabillis	Beauty Bush	1.8 to 2.7 m (6 to 9 ft)	S	pink flowers
Lavateria olbia 'Rosea'	Tree Mallow	1.8 to 2.4 m (6 to 8 ft)	S	soft grey foliage; pink flowers
★*Ligustrum*	Privet	2.1 to 3.3 m (7 to 11 ft)	S	good for hedging
Lonicera	Honeysuckle	2.4 to 4.2 m (8 to 14 ft)	C	fragrant twiner
Malus cvs	Crab Apple	4.5 to 7.5 m (15 to 25 ft)	S	spring blossom; autumn fruit
★*Osmanthus delavayi*	Fragrant Olive	2.4 to 4.5 m (8 to 15 ft)	S	fragrant white flowers
★ *× Osmarea* 'Burwoodii'		1.8 to 3 m (6 to 10 ft)	S	fragrant white flowers
Parthenocissus quinquefolia	Virginia Creeper	6 to 12 m (20 to 40 ft)	C	self clinging; autumn colour
Philadelphus cvs	Mock Orange	1.8 to 4.5 m (6 to 15 ft)	S	fragrant white flowers
★*Phillyrea decora*		2.4 to 4.5 m (8 to 15 ft)	S	small fragrant white flowers; black fruits
Polygonum baldschuanicum	Russian Vine	4.5 to 9 m (15 to 30 ft)	S	vigorous; white flowers
Prunus	Flowering Cherry	2.7 to 7.5 m (9 to 25 ft)	S/U	pink or white flowers
★*Pyracantha*	Firethorn	2.7 to 4.8 m (9 to 16 ft)	S	white flowers; orange berries
Rhus typhina	Stag's Horn Sumach	2.4 to 4.5 m (8 to 15 ft)	S	autumn colour
Ribes sanguineum	Flowering Currant	1.8 to 2.4 m (6 to 8 ft)	U	pink flowers
Rosa cvs	Rose	Variable		wide range of form and flower
Rubus		2.1 to 2.7 m (7 to 9 ft)	S	ornamental brambles
★*Ruscus aculeatus*	Butcher's Broom	1 to 1.5 m (3 to 5 ft)	S	plant male and female bushes for red berries

TREES AND SHRUBS FOR HEAVY SOILS

	COMMON NAME	HEIGHT	HABIT	COMMENTS
Chaenomeles cvs	Flowering Quince, Cydonia	2.1 to 4.5 m (7 to 15 ft)	S	early flowers in shades of pink, red or white
Cornus mas	Cornelian Cherry	4.5 to 7.6 m (15 to 25 ft)	S	yellow flowers before leaves; red fruit
Corylus maxima 'Purpurea'	Purple-leaved Filbert	2.7 to 4.5 m (9 to 15 ft)	S	
Cotinus coggyria	Smoke bush	1.8 to 4.5 m (6 to 15 ft)	S	autumn colour; 'foamy' flower-heads
Crataegus prunifolia		3 to 4.5 m (10 to 15 ft)	S	small tree; fruit
Deutzia cvs		1.2 to 2.1 m (4 to 7 ft)	S	pink or white flowers
Euonymus cvs		45 cm to 2.4 m (1½ to 8 ft)	S	deciduous kinds have good autumn colour
Laburnum	Golden Chain Tree	3.6 to 6 m (12 to 20 ft)	S	pendant clusters of yellow flowers
Philadelphus	Mock Orange	1.8 to 4.5 m (6 to 15 ft)	S	white fragrant flowers
Viburnum		1.2 to 2.1 m (4 to 7 ft)	S	choose deciduous kinds; many have white flowers then berries; autumn colour pink,
Weigela		1.5 to 2.1 m (5 to 7 ft)	S	white or yellow flowers

	COMMON NAME	HEIGHT	HABIT	COMMENTS

TREES AND SHRUBS FOR DRY, SUNNY POSITIONS

	COMMON NAME	HEIGHT	HABIT	COMMENTS
Artemisia abrotanum	Southernwood, Lad's Love	60 cm to 1.2 m (2 to 4 ft)	S	aromatic, silver foliage
★*Berberis*	Barberry	45 cm to 1.9 m (1½ to 6 ft)	S	yellow and orange flowers; red or purple berries
Buddleia cvs	Butterfly Bush	1.8 to 3 m (6 to 10 ft)	S	flowers of various colours attract butterflies
★*Buxus sempervirens*	Box	1 to 2.4 m (3 to 8 ft)	S	slow growing
Caryopteris × *clandonensis* cvs	Blue Spiraea	45 to 75 cm (1½ to 2½ ft)	S	blue flowers late in the season; tolerates chalk
Ceratostigma willmottianum	Hardy Plumbago	38 to 60 cm (15 in to 2 ft)	S	blue flowers
Chaenomeles speciosa cvs	Flowering Quince, Cydonia	2.1 to 4.5 m (7 to 15 ft)	S	early flowers in shades of red pink and white
★*Cistus*	Sun Rose	15 cm to 1.8 m (6 in to 6 ft)	S	pink or white flowers; suitable for seaside; tolerates chalk
★*Convolvulus cneorum*		45 to 60 cm (1½ to 2 ft)	S	silver foliage; white flowers
Cotinus coggygria	Smoke Bush	2.7 to 4.5 m (9 to 15 ft)	S	autumn colour; 'foamy' flower heads
Cytisus cvs	Broom	45 cm to 1.8 m (1½ to 6 ft)	S	flowers white or shades of yellow and red; tolerates lime
★*Erica* cvs	Heather	15 cm to 2.4 m (6 in to 8 ft)	S/U	colour and form according to species and variety
★*Euonymus* cvs		45 cm to 2.4 m (1½ to 8 ft)	S	choose evergreen forms with variegated foliage
Fuchsia cvs		1 to 2.1 (3 to 7 ft)	S	flower colour varies with cv
Genista hispanica	Spanish Gorse	30 to 60 cm (1 to 2 ft)	S	mass of yellow flowers
Hedysarum		1 to 1.2 m (3 to 8 ft)	S	flower colour varies with sp
Hibiscus cvs	Rose Mallow	2.1 to 4.2 m (7 to 14 ft)	U	late flowers in shades of pink, violet and white
★*Hypericum* cvs		15 cm to 1.2 m (6 in to 4 ft)	S	yellow flowers
★*Lavandula* cvs	Lavender	45 cm to 1 m (1½ to 3 ft)	S	aromatic grey foliage; pink or blue flowers
Lavatera olbia	Tree Mallow	1.5 to 2.4 m (5 to 8 ft)	S	soft grey foliage; pink flowers
Lupinus arboreus	Tree Lupin	1.2 to 2.1 m (4 to 7 ft)	S	yellow flowers; suitable for seaside
Lycium barbarum	Duke of Argyll's Tea Tree	1.5 to 2.1 m (5 to 7 ft)	S	purple flowers; spines
★*Olearia*	Daisy Bush	1 to 1.5 m (3 to 5 ft)	S	white daisy flowers; suitable for seaside
Potentilla fruticosa cvs	Shrubby Cinquefoil	45 cm to 1.5 m (15 in to 5 ft)	S	flowers usually yellow
Robina pseudoacacia	False Acacia Tree	9 to 15 m (30 to 50 ft)	U	white flowers
Rosa cvs	Rose	Variable		wide range of form and flower colour; heps
★*Rosmarinus*	Rosemary	15 cm to 1.8 m (6 in to 6 ft)	S/U	aromatic foliage
★*Santolina incana (chamaecyparissus)*	Cotton Lavender	38 cm to 1 m (15 in to 3 ft)	S	silver foliage
★*Senecio* 'Sunshine'		1 to 1.5 m (3 to 5 ft)	S	grey foliage; yellow flowers; suitable for seaside
Spartium junceum	Spanish Broom	1.8 to 2.4 m (6 to 8 ft)	S	yellow flowers; suitable for seaside
★*Tamarix tetrandra*	Tamarisk	2.4 to 3.6 m (8 to 12 ft)	S	small pink flowers; suitable for seaside
Ulex europaeus	Gorse	1.2 to 2.4 m (4 to 8 ft)	S	yellow flowers; suitable for seaside
★*Vinca*	Periwinkle	10 to 15 cm (4 to 6 in)	S	mauve or white flowers; creeping habit
★*Yucca*		1.5 to 3 m (5 to 10 ft)	U	tall cream flower spike; suitable for seaside

SHRUBS FOR SHADED WALLS

	COMMON NAME	HEIGHT	HABIT	COMMENTS
★*Camellia* cvs		1.5 to 2.4 m (5 to 8 ft)	S	flowers white or shades of pink, varied in form; lime-free soil
Chaenomeles speciosa cvs	Flowering Quince, Cydonia	2.1 to 4.5 m (7 to 15 ft)	S	early flowers in shade of pink, red or white
Clematis montana		6 to 9 m (20 to 30 ft)	C	pink flowers
Cotoneaster horizontalis		3.6 to 4.5 m (12 to 15 ft)	S	red berries; good wall shrub
Hydrangea petiolaris	Climbing hydrangea	9 to 15 m (30 to 50 ft)	C	self clinging
Jasminum nudiflorum	Winter Jasmine	4.5 to 6 m (15 to 20 ft)	C	yellow flowers in winter
★*Pyracantha*	Firethorn	2.7 to 4.8 m (9 to 16 ft)	S	white flowers; orange berries

TREES AND SHRUBS FOR SHADY POSITIONS

	COMMON NAME	HEIGHT	HABIT	COMMENTS
★*Arundinaria*	Bamboo	3 to 4.5 m (10 to 15 ft)	S	
★*Aucuba japonica* cvs	Spotted Laurel	1.5 to 2.7 m (5 to 9 ft)	S	
★*Berberis*	Barberry	45 cm to 1.8 m (1½ to 6 ft)	S	yellow or orange flowers; red or purple fruit
★*Camellia* cvs		1.5 to 2.4 m (5 to 8 ft)	S	flowers white or shades of pink, varied in form; lime-free soil
Chaenomeles speciosa cvs	Flowering Quince, Cydonia	2.1 to 4.5 m (7 to 15 ft)	S	early flowers in shades of pink, red or white

	COMMON NAME	HEIGHT	HABIT	COMMENTS
Clethra alnifolia	Sweet Pepper Bush	1.5 to 2.7 m (5 to 9 ft)	S	white fragrant flowers
Cornus alba 'Sibirica'	Westonbirt Dogwood	1.2 to 2.4 m (4 to 8 ft)	S	bright red winter stems
Corylopsis	Winter Hazel	1 to 4.5 m (3 to 15 ft)	S	pale yellow, fragrant flowers appear before foliage
Cotoneaster horizontalis		30 to 38 cm (12 to 15 in)	S	red berries
★*Danae racemosa*	Alexandrian Laurel	60 cm to 1 m (2 to 3 ft)	S	
Daphne mezereum	Mezereon	1.5 to 2.9 m (5 to 8 ft)	S	pink flowers; poisonous fruits
Deutzia cvs		1.2 to 2.1 m (4 to 7 ft)	S	pink or white flowers
Disanthus cercidifolius		2.1 to 4.5 m (7 to 15 ft)	S	autumn colour
★*Elaeagnus*		1.2 to 2.7 m (6 to 9 ft)	S	suitable for seaside
Enkianthus campanulatus		2.1 to 2.7 m (7 to 9 ft)	S	lime-free soil
Euonymus alatus	Spindle berry	2.1 to 2.7 m (7 to 9 ft)	S	autumn colour
★*Fatsia japonica*	Fig Leaf Palm	1.2 to 2.1 m (4 to 7 ft)	S	white flowers; large lobed leaves
★*Gaultheria shallon*		1.5 to 2.1 m (5 to 7 ft)	S	pale pink flowers; purple fruits
★*Hedera cvs*	Ivy	4.5 to 12 m (15 to 40 ft)	C	many cvs have variegated foliage
Hydrangea		60 cm to 2.7 m (2 to 9 ft)	S	pink or blue flowers according to soil
★*Hypericum calycinum*	Rose of Sharon	15 to 23 cm (6 to 9 in)	S	vigorous ground coverer; yellow flowers
★*Leucothoe catesbaei (fontanesiana)*		1 to 1.8 m (3 to 6 ft)	S	ground coverer for lime-free soils; white flowers
★*Mahonia cvs*		45 cm to 1.5 m (1½ to 5 ft)	S	yellow flowers in winter and early spring
★*Pachysandra terminalis*		15 to 23 cm (6 to 9 in)	S	
★*Pieris cvs*	Lily-of-the-valley Tree	1.8 to 6 m (6 to 20 ft)	S	several cvs have young red foliage
★*Pyracantha*	Firethorn	2.7 to 4.8 m (9 to 16 ft)	S	white flowers; orange berries
★*Rhododendron cvs*		30 cm to 6 m (1 to 20 ft)	S/U	lime-free soil
Rubus		1 to 2.7 m (3 to 9 ft)	S	ornamental brambles
★*Sarcococca*	Christmas Box	38 to 60 cm (15 in to 2 ft)	S	
★*Skimmia cvs*		1 to 1.5 m (3 to 5 ft)	S	plant male and female plants for red berries
Symphoricarpos	Snowberry	1.2 to 1.8 m (4 to 6 ft)	S	white or pink berries
Vaccinium corymbosum	High-bush Blueberry	1.5 to 1.8 m (5 to 6 ft)	S	lime-free soil; edible berries

TREES AND SHRUBS FOR TOWN GARDENS

	COMMON NAME	HEIGHT	HABIT	COMMENTS
Acer cvs	Maple	1.2 to 15 m (4 to 50 ft)	S/U	autumn colour
Aesculus hippocastanum	Horse Chestnut	12 to 18 m (40 to 60 ft)	S	white 'candles'; conkers
Ailanthus altissima	Tree-of-heaven	15 to 21 m (50 to 70 ft)	U	red, wing-like fruits on female trees
Berberis (Deciduous kinds)	Barberry	45 cm to 1.8 m (1½ to 6 ft)	S	yellow or orange flowers; red or purple berries
Betula	Birch	3.6 to 4.5 m (12 to 15 ft)	S/U	attractive bark
Buddleia cvs	Butterfly Bush	1.8 to 3 m (6 to 10 ft)	S	flowers attract butterflies
Chaenomeles cvs	Flowering Quince, Cydonia	2.1 to 4.5 m (7 to 15 ft)	S	early flowers in shades of pink, red or white
Cotoneaster (deciduous kinds)		45 cm to 2.4 m (15 in to 8 ft)	S	red berries
Crataegus		4.5 to 7.6 m (15 to 25 ft)		haws and autumn colour
Daphne mezereum	Mezereon	1.5 to 2.4 m (5 to 8 ft)	S	pink flowers, poisonous fruits
Deutzia cvs		1.2 to 2.1 m (4 to 7 ft)	S	pink or white flowers
★*Euonymus fortunei radicans*		15 to 30 cm (6 to 12 in)	S	will trail or climb
★*Fatsia japonica*	Fig-leaf Palm	1.2 to 2.1 m (4 to 7 ft)	S	white flowers; large, lobed leaves
Forsythia		2.1 to 4.5 m (7 to 15 ft)	S	yellow flowers
Hebe brachysiphon (traversii)		1.2 to 1.5 m (4 to 5 ft)	S	suitable for seaside; white flowers
★*Hedera cvs*	Ivy	4.5 to 12 m (15 to 40 ft)	C	many cvs have variegated foliage
Hibiscus cvs	Rose Mallow	2.1 to 4.2 m (7 to 14 ft)	U	late flowers in shades of pink, violet and white
Hypericum cvs		15 cm to 1.2 m (6 in to 4 ft)	S	yellow flowers
★*Jasminum nudiflorum*	Winter Jasmine	2.4 to 4.2 m (8 to 14 ft)	C	yellow winter flowers
Kerria japonica 'Pleniflora'	Jew's Mallow	1.2 to 1.8 m (4 to 6 ft)	S	green stems; yellow flowers
Laburnum × watereri 'Vossii'	Golden Chain Tree	3.6 to 6 m (12 to 20 ft)	U	clusters of yellow flowers
★*Ligustrum*	Privet	2.1 to 3.3 m (7 to 11 ft)	S	
★*Mahonia cvs*		45 cm to 1.5 m (1½ to 15 ft)	S	yellow flowers in winter and early spring
Malus cvs	Crab Apple	4.5 to 7.6 m (15 to 25 ft)	S	spring blossom; autumn fruit
★*Olearia × haastii*	Daisy Bush	1.2 to 1.8 m (4 to 6 ft)	S	white flowers
Parthenocissus quinquefolia	Virginia Creeper	3.6 to 12 m (12 ft to 40 ft)	C	self-clinging; autumn colour
★*Pernettya*	Prickly Heath	60 cm to 1.5 m (2 to 5 ft)	S	white flowers; brilliant berries
Philadelphus cvs	Mock Orange	1.8 to 4.5 m (6 to 15 ft)	S	white fragrant flowers
Prunus cvs	Flowering Cherries	2.7 to 7.6 m (9 to 25 ft)	S/U	pink or white blossom
★*Pyracantha*	Firethorn	2.7 to 4.8 m (9 to 16 ft)	S	white flowers; orange berries
Rhus typhina	Stag's Horn Sumach	2.4 to 4.5 m (8 to 15 ft)	S	autumn colour
Ribes sanguineum	Flowering Currant	1.8 to 2.4 m (5 to 8 ft)	U	pink flowers
Rosa cvs	Rose	Variable		wide range of form and flower
★*Senecio* 'Sunshine'		1 to 1.5 m (3 to 5 ft)★	S	grey foliage; yellow flowers; suitable for seaside
Sorbus		75 cm to 7.6 m (2½ to 25 ft)	U	
Spiraea cvs		45 cm to 1.2 m (1½ to 4 ft)	S	graceful flowering shrubs
Syringa cvs	Lilac	45 cm to 3 m (1½ to 10 ft)	S/U	flowers in shades of pink, mauve and white

	COMMON NAME	HEIGHT	HABIT	COMMENTS
Viburnum		1.2 to 2.1 m (4 to 7 ft)	S	varied genus; many have white flowers followed by berries
★Vinca	Periwinkle	10 to 15 cm (4 to 6 in)	S	mauve or white flowers; creeping
Weigela		1.5 to 2.1 m (5 to 7 ft)	S	pink, white or yellow flowers
★Yucca		1.8 to 3 m (6 to 10 ft)	S	tall cream flower spike; suitable for seaside

GROUND COVER PLANTS

	COMMON NAME	HABIT	COMMENTS
Ajuga reptans 'Multicolor'	Bugle	I, D	colourful variegated foliage
Alchemilla mollis	Lady's Mantle	S, O	small sulphur-yellow flowers
Anaphalis	Pearl Everlasting	S	silver foliage; white flowers
Anemone japonica	Japanese Anemone	S	pink flowers
Artemisia		O	silver foliage
Aruncus sylvester	Goat's Beard	U	white plume-like flowers
Asperula odorata	Woodruff	I, D	fragrant grey foliage
Astilbe cvs	False Goat's Beard	U	plume-like flower spikes in red, pink and white
★Bergenia cvs	Elephant's Ears	S, D	early pink flowers
Calluna cvs	Scottish Ling	S, O	many cvs of varied foliage and flower colour
Campanula portenschlagiana	Bellflower	I	blue-mauve flowers
Centaurea dealbata	Knapwood	O	pink flowers
Cerastium tomentosum	Snow-in-summer	S, O	silver foliage; white flowers
★*Cistus × pulverulentus*		S	bright pink flowers
Convallaria majalis	Lily-of-the-valley	I, D	white fragrant flowers
Cornus canadensis	Creeping Dogwood	I, D	white flowers; red fruits
★*Cotoneaster dammeri* 'Skogsholm'		S, D	red berries
Cyclamen neapolitanum (hederifolium)		I, D	marbled foliage; pink flowers
★*Daboecia cantabrica* cvs	St Daboec's Heath	O	pink flowers; lime-free soil
Dicentra oregana		I	pale yellow flowers
Dryopteris		S, D	easy-to-grow ferns
Epimedium	Barrenwort	I, D	attractive flowers; decorative foliage
★Erica cvs	Heather	S, O	flowers and foliage vary with sp and cv
★*Euonymus fortunei radicans*		S, O	
★*Euphorbia robbiae*	Spurge	I, D	sulphur-yellow flowers
★*Festuca glauca*	Blue Grass	I, O	
★*Gaultheria procumbens*	Checkerberry	I, D	bright red fruits in winter
★*Gaultheria shallon*		S, D	pale pink flowers; purple fruits
Geranium	Crane's Bill	S, O, D	flowers pink or mauve
Genista hispanica	Spanish Gorse	S, O	yellow flowers
★*Hebe pinguifolia* 'Pagei'	Shrubby Speedwell	S	green-grey foliage; white flowers
★Hedera cvs	Ivy	I, D	Many cvs have variegated foliage
Helianthemum cvs	Rock Rose	S, O	wide range of flower colours
★Helleborus	Hellebore	D	fine foliage; greenish flowers
Hosta cvs	Plantain Lily	D	wide range of foliage colour
Hydrangea petiolaris	Climbing Hydrangea	I	covers a steep bank as well as it covers a wall
★*Hypericum calycinum*	Rose of Sharon	I, D	large yellow flowers
★*Lamium galeobdolan*	Yellow Dead Nettle	I, D	
★Lavandula cvs	Lavender	S	pink or mauve flowers; aromatic foliage
Luzula maxima	Creeping Woodrush	D	grass-like foliage
★*Mahonia aquifolium*	Oregon Grape	I, D	early yellow flowers; blue berries
Nepeta mussinii	Catmint	S, O	grey foliage; mauve flowers
Oxalis magellanica		I, D	
★*Pachysandra terminalis*		I, D	
Polygonum vaccinifolium		S, O	pink flowers
Pulmonaria	Lungwort	I	
Rodgersia		D	handsome foliage
★*Rubus tricolor*		I	trailing stems; white flowers
Salvia	Sage	S, O	purple and golden-leaved forms available
★*Santolina incana (chamaecyparissus)*	Cotton Lavender	S, O	silver foliage
★*Sarcococca hookerana digyna*		S	white flowers; black berries
Saxifraga	Saxifrage	I	large and varied genus
★Senecio 'Sunshine'		S	yellow flowers; grey foliage
★*Stachys lanata*	Lamb's Ear	S, O	soft felted foliage
★*Symphytum grandiflorum*	Comfrey	I, D	purple flowers
Tellima grandiflora		I, D	bronzy foliage
Tiarella cordifolia	Foam Flower	I, D	cream flower spike
Trachystemon orientale		I, D	violet flower spikes
★*Vinca minor*	Periwinkle	I, D	mauve flowers
★*Viburnum davidii*		S	plant male and female plants for turquoise berries
Viola ladradorica	Violet	I	blue flowers

BIBLIOGRAPHY

Beazley, Elizabeth: *Design and Detail of the Space between Buildings.* Architectural Press, London 1962
Beckett, Carr, & Stevens: *The Contained Garden.* Frances Lincoln, London 1982
Brookes, John: *Room Outside.* Thames and Hudson, London 1969
Brookes, Lane-Fox, & Hellyer: *The Financial Times Book of Garden Design.* David and Charles, Newton Abbot 1975
Hay, Roy & Synge, Patrick M.: *The Dictionary of Garden Plants in Colour.* Michael Joseph, London 1969
Hellyer, Arthur: *The Collingridge Illustrated Encyclopedia of Gardening.* Newnes Books, Twickenham 1982 (Revised edition)
Hilliers Manual of Trees and Shrubs. David and Charles, Newton Abbot 1974
Huxley, Anthony: *An Illustrated History of Gardening.* Macmillan, London 1978
Jellicoe, Susan & Allen, Marjory: *Town Gardens to Live In.* Penguin Books, London 1977
Stevens, David: *Making a Garden.* Worlds Works, Tadworth 1984
Saville, Diana: *Walled Gardens.* Batsford, London 1982
Wood, Dennis: *Terrace and Courtyard Designs.* David and Charles, Newton Abbot 1970

INDEX